STUDYING THE NEW TESTAMENT

Bruce Chilton is the Bernard Iddings Bell Professor of Religion at Bard College, New York, and is the author of numerous books, including *Abraham's Curse: The Roots of Violence in Judaism, Christianity, and Islam; Rabbi Jesus: An Intimate Biography;* and *Rabbi Paul: An Intellectual Biography.*

Deirdre Good is Professor of New Testament at General Theological Seminary, New York, and is the author of several books, including *Jesus' Family Values* and *Jesus the Meek King.*

STUDYING
THE NEW TESTAMENT

A Fortress Introduction

BRUCE CHILTON

DEIRDRE GOOD

FORTRESS PRESS
MINNEAPOLIS

STUDYING THE NEW TESTAMENT
A Fortress Introduction

Fortress Press Edition 2011

Copyright © 2009 Bruce Chilton and Deirdre Good

Cover image: Images of the Communion of Saints tapestries created by John Nava for the Cathedral of Our Lady of the Angels, Los Angeles, California.
Cover design: Laurie Ingram

Library of Congress Cataloging-in-Publication Data
Chilton, Bruce.
  Studying the New Testament : a Fortress introduction / Bruce Chilton, Deirdre J. Good.
    p. cm.
  Originally published : London : Society for Promoting Christian Knowledge, c2009.
  Includes bibliographical references and index.
  ISBN 978-0-8006-9735-8 (alk. paper)
  1. Bible. N.T.—Introductions. I. Good, Deirdre Joy. II. Title.
  BS2330.3.C53 2011
  225.6'1—dc22
                                        2010018955

Manufactured in the U.S.A.

16 15 14 13 12 11   1 2 3 4 5 6 7 8 9 10

Contents

List of maps, figures, boxes, and tables

Tables

Preface

This book began as a revision of an earlier volume, *Beginning New Testament Study* (London: SPCK, 1986). In the process of the revision, the authors and Rebecca Mulhearn, their editor at SPCK, realized that more than twenty years of change since *Beginning New Testament Study* appeared necessitated a different approach and an entirely new text, so much so that this is very much a new book.

The original volume was valued for offering, not another conventional New Testament introduction, but a way into understanding the kind of literature it is and how it could be studied. In order to achieve that aim today, we decided that further discussion of each book of the New Testament within a historical context needed to be provided, and that bibliography, exercises and notes needed to be offered for those embarking on an academic course of study. A more detailed discussion of individual books is provided in *The Cambridge Companion to the Bible*, second edition (Bruce Chilton, with contributions from Howard Clark Kee, Eric M. Meyers, John Rogerson, Amy-Jill Levine, Anthony J. Saldarini, Cambridge: Cambridge University Press, 2008). But in the balance of parts and the whole that we believe is key to serious study, we hope that our readers are here given a good start.

Resources made available to us by Fortress Press, for which we are grateful to our editor, Ross Miller, have enabled us to extend our approach. We hope that readers will appreciate new illustrations, a comprehensive system of referring to all visual representations in the book, and an electronic companion (www.fortresspress. com/chiltongood). These enhancements are intended to enliven the presentation, and to enable students to pursue their interests further into some of the resources, written and archaeological, which illuminate the New Testament and its world in ways that scarcely could have been imagined even a few decades ago.

Introduction

For nearly two thousand years, both believers and non-believers have grappled with the New Testament. What exactly does it say? Why do its authors claim divine status for Jesus? Do they mean to speak literally of the end of the world?

These and other questions were posed even before the time all the 27 books of the New Testament were written. During the period when the great majority of Jesus' followers were illiterate, teachers and new believers alike had to rely on oral tradition. Because they saw their tradition as sacred, their own acute interest – and their personal interpretations – shaped what they handed on to their followers. We possess nothing Jesus wrote, since he was in all probability illiterate, but much that he said. Jesus' sayings and actions were transmitted through gospels, letters and sermons in contexts that described his life and death for contemporaries. So the way the New Testament came into being actually invites and encourages further interpretation.

The purpose of this book, as its title says, is to help the reader make a start in the critical study of the New Testament. To achieve that objective, we as authors need to accomplish two aims. The challenging dimension of our task is that we need to accomplish both aims at once.

Any curious reader of the New Testament, no matter what his or her attitude, whether motivated by faith or by secular considerations, needs to balance a familiarity with the specifics of the 27 books of the New Testament with the cumulative impact of the message of the New Testament as a whole. The whole and its parts are constantly in dialog in one's mind in the course of any serious reading. Addressing that tension is our first challenge.

For that reason, we have decided to offer our readers a narrative description of the development of the New Testament, introducing key themes and delving into the social worlds in which the texts emerged. That narrative must begin before the texts themselves were produced, with a consideration of Jesus and the movement he founded and inspired (Chapter 1). Because Jesus consciously developed a program of action for his followers, as well as featuring as the center of their devotion at a later stage, we prefer to speak of 'Jesus' movement' rather than of 'the Jesus movement'. Then, in chronological order, we treat the letters of Paul, and Paul himself as Christianity's first public intellectual (Chapter 2). A consideration of the Gospels follows, because they emerged after the time of Paul and reflect a period of considerable growth of Jesus' movement in the Mediterranean world a full generation after his death (Chapter 3). Finally, the last chapter treats the writings that complete the New Testament, a combination of books that address the emerging Church at large and deal with questions of how the teaching of Jesus fits into the whole pattern of world history (Chapter 4).

By approaching the New Testament along the lines of how its development unfolded, we hope to give our readers a sense of the environment within which each of the 27 books was produced. But that development is not merely a question of the individual histories of those books. Coherent principles, whether implicit or explicit, were also involved.

Among the implicit principles, Jesus' teachings and actions, although they were not a matter of public record at the time he lived, formed a standard of his followers' faith and ethics. Paul's teaching was by no means accepted by a majority of believers during his life, but nonetheless came to provide non-Jewish Christians with a sense of how they could belong to Jesus' movement. The Gospels represent the broad commitment of Jesus' movement to educating and advancing believers in the significance of their faith, while the last writings of the New Testament raise concerns about the content of faith and its relationship to other forms of thought, such as philosophy and history.

The explicit principles that determined which works would be included in the New Testament were (1) whether they were understood to derive from one of the groups of the apostles, those delegated by Jesus to deliver his message, and (2) whether they were accepted broadly by the Church as a whole. The first principle meant that from the early days of Christianity believers concerned themselves with historical questions regarding how a given document emerged. The second principle committed Christians to a concern for whether, in addition to being originally connected to Jesus, a document was 'catholic', that is, universally recognized (*katholikos*). These principles have been named since the second century of the Common Era, when the New Testament as we would recognize it was widely accepted. The actual listing of a table of contents that agrees with ours was finalized during the fourth century.

By attending historically to how the individual books of the New Testament were generated in their times, and fit into a pattern that focused on Jesus, Paul, the communities of the Gospels, and writings to the Catholic Church after the Gospels, we believe that a sense of the whole of the New Testament and its parts will come home to our readers. As we go through this development, we also offer advice on how to move beyond the phase of starting study into study itself. That is our second challenge.

Serious reading of the New Testament will always involve balancing the whole and the parts, but readers will need more detailed advice about the nuts and bolts of texts, as well as about the wider task of interpretation, in order to move ahead. We aim to provide readers with what they need by means of explanatory material within chapters, and exercises after each chapter that are intended to encourage the reader to engage closely with the texts and to build awareness of and confidence in some of the scholarly issues.

As we do so, we call attention to basic methods of study.

Source criticism

Behind every text lie earlier traditions of some kind. Source criticism seeks to identify these earlier traditions and probe how they are used in the present text since this may well reveal an author's intentions and purpose for writing. As well as finding sources of the text, source criticism tries to determine textual relationships among similar texts and directions of dependence. Source critics propose to isolate materials of different style and vocabulary from a text, arguing that they belong to a different source.

Social-scientific theory

From the social sciences come questions about the social, historical and cultural dimensions of a text inhabiting a pre-industrial world very different from ours. In regard to the social world of the first century, social sciences propose to clarify organizational structures, kinship systems, family relations, purity and pollution taboos, lineage and inheritance, and economical and political structures. The pre-industrial agrarian world of the first century differs from ours in that 90 per cent of ancient society at the time of the New Testament lived in a rural environment, engaged in farming at a subsistence level. Only 2–4 per cent of the population were literate. Life expectancy was about half of ours, and households with widows and children were not uncommon. New Testament writers presume their readers belong to ancient Mediterranean society and share a social system in which the group is valued over the individual and a premium is placed on honor and avoidance of shame. Slavery is normative. A system of patrons and clients makes things work.

Redaction and tradition criticism

Redaction criticism identifies the way editors (redactors) adapt and arrange source materials in the text they are creating. By identifying these alterations and arrangements in the text, redaction critics try to identify the interests of an author and an author's community. Redaction critics engage with literary approaches to the documents they study, in order to appreciate the theologies that the editors espoused, and how their ideas and beliefs influenced their presentation of the traditional materials known to them. The method necessarily confronts the question of the shape and content of traditions included in the work of redactors. In pursuing that issue, redaction criticism can develop into tradition criticism, intersecting with the identification of sources. But the individual traditions incorporated in a document need not be identifiable with a particu-lar source. Sometimes, the form of a tradition indicates its purpose and provenance. The pursuit of those issues is characteristic of form criticism. Redaction criticism begins with texts as we have them, as the work of editors or authors (sometimes working cooperatively). Once the preferences of these contributors are known, in terms of style, theology and content, it is possible to dig deeper, into the preferences of earlier sources, individual traditions and oral collections of material.

Reader-response criticism

A text has a life of its own, independent of its author, and often with a multiplicity of meanings. And what about the reader? Reader-oriented theories recognize that readers bring to the text different worlds of experience and presuppositions. Such interpretative worlds bring out what is latent in the text. The text has no inherent meaning; indeed, some scholars assert that it is the reader who creates textual meaning. A modified version of this approach would be that meaning comes from engagement between the reader and the text rather than from discerning the intention of the author. Into this meeting-place of author and text, scholars have identified central interpretative questions to address: the social location of the author and reader including a reader's race, class and gender, ideologies of authors and interpreters, the nature of language.

Perhaps it is in the intersection of author, reader and text that interpretation best takes place. When we engage in a dialog with another person, we attend not just to what their language conveys but to the way words are communicated: the phrasing and choice of words, and the inflection of voice and facial expressions, for example. As a dialog partner, we can ask the speaker for clarification. We can also take into account circumstances in which the conversation took place and what we know of the author's own world at that particular time.

In the case of the biblical text, although the author is no longer available to be questioned, the world of the author is. Meaning may be derived from an investigation of what the author of a biblical text intends to convey, alongside what the text articulates, and how the reader perceives the text. To emphasize author, reader or text at the expense of one of the other three is to impoverish the process of interpretation.

As readers proceed into a study of the New Testament, they engage in both exegesis, the identification of meaning as it comes out of the wording of a text, and interpretation, the synthesis of that meaning within an understanding of our world as a whole.

The aim of exegesis is to make explicit the possible particular meanings of the words and ideas in a text. Exegesis is the basis of interpretation. Interpretation cannot exist except as engaging with exegesis. This occurs when the connotations of words and concepts are explained as fully as possible and when the text is placed in the context of the presuppositions, questions and concerns of its author, community or tradition. Since an author uses language to shape the text, an exegete must attend first to aspects of the Greek language behind the New Testament, including morphology (word forms), lexicology (meaning) and syntax (word relationships).

Readers familiar with the thought system of the text they are reading are able to partner with the text in looking at reality with different eyes. But if readers are no longer part of the thought system of the text, as would be the case with us and ancient texts, they can recreate a framework of meaning from the text, uncover shortcomings and discover dormant alternative answers in the text. Historical distance does not reduce the effectiveness of a text: it can encourage the production of meaning that enables moderns to overcome their own thought system and broaden their reality.

Interpretation involves creating present meaning for an ancient text. While it used to be thought possible to uncover an author's original objective meaning, such interpretations were found to reflect rather too much of the interpreter's perspective. Freeing the text of author and context was one way to address an impasse. Another way is to work with original languages through historical research. Reader-oriented interpretation also opened up the text to address and be accountable to the present. We propose to take none of these approaches in isolation but to value a dynamic between author, text and reader, balancing each and even stressing one but never losing sight of all three in interpretative activity. The text is living and elusive. Its words always lie beyond our reach, reminding us of the unfinished challenge of interpretation.

Bibliographical background

Many comprehensive introductions to the New Testament are available. Among those recently published, we recommend Raymond E. Brown, *An Introduction to the New Testament* (New York: Doubleday, 1997). Brown's work represents a renewed historical interest in the study of the New Testament, after several decades in which theories of interpretation sometimes eclipsed history.

Nonetheless, Brown's approach needs to be supplemented by a knowledge of methods of study, and the theories behind those methods. For that reason, we recommend the work of Paul Gooder (ed.), *Searching for Meaning: An Introduction to Interpreting the New Testament* (London: SPCK and Louisville, Kentucky: Westminster John Knox, 2008). The social constituencies involved in the production of the New Testament are the particular concern of Howard Clark Kee, *The Beginnings of Christianity: An Introduction to the New Testament* (New York: T. &T. Clark, 2005).

The approach we take in this volume is not confessional, and does not ask the reader to assent from the beginning to the message of the New Testament. During the period in scholarship when theoretical approaches took precedence over historical approaches, an attempt grew to insist on belief as a condition of understanding the texts. Examples of this view include Brevard S. Childs, *The New Testament as Canon: An Introduction* (Philadelphia: Fortress, 1985) and, more recently, Luke Timothy Johnson, *The Writings of the New Testament: An Interpretation* (Minneapolis: Augsburg Fortress, 1999; Third Edition, 2010). In our view, a properly historical approach informs issues of faith, but does not determine a reader's decisions in that regard.

Dictionaries, translations, commentaries and websites

Dictionaries

The semantic world of the New Testament is completely different from linguistic worlds of the modern reader. Lexicons and dictionaries open up the surprising language world of the New Testament. For example, the third edition of Walter Bauer's *A Greek–English Lexicon of the New Testament and Other Early Christian Literature*, edited and revised by Frederick William Danker and published in 2000 by the University of Chicago Press, is a landmark publication. It clarifies Greek words through extended meanings. While older dictionaries provided equivalents for Greek words (*logos* = word), this new edition of Bauer contains entries that supply extended interpretations of words rather than word-for-word substitutes (glosses).

Concordances and exegetical dictionaries are also useful. Concordances list all instances of Hebrew or Greek words behind English translations. They enable investigators to work with a range of connotations for a particular entry. Interpreters working with lexicons and dictionaries should note that sometimes lexicon and dictionary writers are inclined to compile information about the entire history of the interpretation of a particular word in one single entry. This is not necessarily relevant to the occurrence of a word in a particular passage and, if imported wholesale, and may lead to erroneous assumptions. 'Theological Word Books' can overlay words with theological connotations not present in particular instances. A good rule of thumb is to interpret words within the larger context of the text in which they occur, rather than as they appear in a completely different writing.

Of course, no word exists in isolation. Words and phrases combine to form sentences, paragraphs and whole texts. Analysing sentence structure is essential to grasp grammar and syntax, ideally on the basis of the Greek text. Grammatical analysis however is only the starting-point.

9

Translations

All translation is interpretation. If I am translating your speech into, say, French, and you use the word 'word', I must interpret whether the appropriate equivalent is 'mot' or 'parole'.

All translations of the New Testament, whether done by individuals or commissioned by national committees, are interpretations. Confronted by a range of Bibles on the shelves of a library or on the worldwide web, a person wanting to borrow from or read a Bible must make a selection. Which one is the best? How do I choose between the different translations? Of Bible translations there is no end in sight. A modern reader has to assess critically each translation. Some translations have different purposes: the English Authorized Version of 1611 represents a move away from an essentially privatized reading of Scripture through a translation designed to enhance the spoken literary character of the text. Attention to public reading of the text continues in the Revised Standard Version and the New Revised Standard Version translations. The NRSV is authorized for use in Protestant churches today. It is also a response to the issue of inclusive language by trying to render language about human beings inclusively. Publishers are also printing translations of the Bible by individuals: Everett Fox has almost completed a translation of the Hebrew Bible that presents both the literal meaning and the structural form of the Hebrew; Eugene H. Peterson, at the other end of the scale, published his 2003 translation, *The Message*, in contemporary idiomatic middle-class language.

Bible sales today represent a large market – estimated between $425 million (by HarperSanFrancisco) and $609 million (by Zondervan), with relatively stable sales. So the publishing industry also promotes new translations and markets them.

The preface of a Bible translation states the translation's philosophy. All translators choose words and ideas to render the underlying Greek, Hebrew and Aramaic texts. There is rarely an exact equivalent for each word, and the particular syntax of the source language may influence meaning in a way that is hard to render in a target language, such as English.

There are two basic translation theories in evidence today: the formal equivalence model and the dynamic equivalence model. All translations fall somewhere on a sliding scale between these two options. Translators using a formal equivalence model try to render the original into English so as to reflect the philological root meaning and the syntactic patterns of the source language; the end result may seem strange to modern ears since the source text comes from a linguistic, social and cultural world that is profoundly different from our own. Translations made using the dynamic equivalence model try to render the source text into familiar modern language. If an idiomatic expression is used in the Greek, a dynamic equivalence translation will render it into an equivalent current English idiom, rather than trying to reflect the literal equivalence of the words and the form of the expression. In Matthew's parable about the labourers in the vineyard, labourers who have worked all day complain because the landowner has paid workers employed at the end of the day the same wage. Let's look at the landowner's response in Matthew 20.15. A literal translation would be a 'or the eye of you evil is it because good am I?' In a formal equivalence translation we find 'Is your eye evil because I am good?' In a dynamic equivalence translation, here the NRSV, Jesus says: 'Or are you envious because I am generous?' This translation is more familiar language to modern ears, but it loses a number of original features which would have been noticed by an audience: the connection with eye imagery, the discussion of who or what is good elsewhere in Matthew, and, to some of us, the strangeness of the 'evil eye' language. Only an annotated NRSV includes the formal equivalence translation in a footnote; a translation without scholarly notes will not alert the reader (or listener) to an 'evil eye'. Footnotes might note that throughout the Ancient Near East and in many cultures today, people believe an 'evil eye' can do harm; in Matthew 20.15 it describes a greedy, not generous outlook.

The King James Version, now rather outdated in terms of translation theory and textual criticism, nevertheless does an admirable job of providing a formal equivalence translation, and it is important to read it next to modern translations, especially to balance the modern tendency to favor dynamic equivalence over formal equivalence. We have already observed the fact that translations are meant to be read out loud in worship services. Translations using principles of dynamic equivalence likely to be licensed for reading in the churches of different religious bodies must contain a coherent text. Annotated Bibles relegate comments like 'Greek obs(cure)' or 'meaning unknown' to footnotes rather than printing gaps or question marks in the text. But if textual interpretation is the goal, then gaps, obscurities and conjectured readings must be noted somewhere.

Commentaries

All interpretations of the New Testament, past or present, contribute to an explanation of what it means. Because there are so many interpretations and will be even more in the future, any interpretation, whether past or present, will have to be understood as provisional or contingent. Academic scholars have, until recently, privileged post-Enlightenment twentieth-century and subsequent readings and interpretations of the New Testament, on the grounds that serious critical study is a recent phenomenon. In fact, published scholarship until quite recently has been, and in some places continues to be, supercessionist: it presumes that the most recent interpretation, the one it is currently creating, is correct. Older interpretations from earliest times to the Middle Ages and up until the Enlightenment were thought quaint and mostly irrelevant. But most scholars now recognize different historical and cultural specificities of the various books of the New Testament and the influence of historical and cultural situations on every reader of biblical texts. It seems obvious that all people are products of their environment and the time and communities in which they live. So if all readings of the New Testament are culturally specific, and no single particular reading privileged over another, then attending to readings of other individuals and communities is essential. Thus more recent scholarship acknowledges all patristic, medieval and pre-Enlightenment interpretations as essential contributions to New Testament interpretation by finding and engaging with them, asking questions like, 'How do they interpret the New Testament?' rather than, 'Are they right?'

While it might be easy to find biblical interpretations preserved in collections, for example, that of the Church Fathers, locating and reading material other than commentaries takes time. What is in print is likely to be the work of trained scholars. Michael Cahill argues that a seventh-century Latin text written by an Irish monk is the first commentary on Mark's Gospel. While the Latin text has existed for some time, Cahill published a critical English edition and translation (1998).

Websites

The internet is an ever-changing entity, with some websites there one day and gone the next. Listed below are a few reliable and helpful websites that have (so far) stood the test of time.

- <http://www.ntgateway.com/>

Compiled by Mark Goodacre, Associate Professor in New Testament at the Department of Religion, Duke University, this is an excellent and up-to-date portal for all things New Testament.

- <http://www.perseus.tufts.edu/hopper/>

This site is from the Department of Classics at Tuft University, and is good for history, literature and culture of the Graeco-Roman world (including online hypertext dictionaries).

- <http://pace.mcmaster.ca/York/york/index.htm>

Steve Mason's PACE (Project on Ancient Cultural Engagement) includes links to the texts of Josephus; although the translation is old it is a good place to start for information about Josephus.

- <http://ocp.acadiau.ca/>

The Online Critical Pseudepigrapha is an electronic publication of the Society of Biblical Literature and aims to develop and publish electronic editions of the best critical texts of the 'Old Testament' Pseudepigrapha and related literature.

Further reading

Gordon Fee and Mark Strauss, *How to Choose a Translation for All Its Worth: A Guide to Understanding and Using Bible Versions* (Grand Rapids, Michigan: Zondervan, 2004)

A Greek–English Lexicon of the New Testament and Other Early Christian Literature (3rd edn, Chicago: University of Chicago Press, 2000)

Books of the New Testament

The dates at which New Testament books were written continue to be debated by scholars. The following is the order in which many, but not all, scholars believe they were most likely written, with approximate dates:

The First Letter to the Thessalonians, 50 C.E.
The Letter to the Galatians, 53 C.E.
The First Letter to the Corinthians, 55 C.E.
The Second Letter to the Corinthians, 56 C.E.
The Letter to the Romans, 57 C.E.
The Letter to Philemon, 58 C.E.
The Letter to the Philippians, 62 C.E.
The Letter to the Colossians (at its earliest stage), 62 C.E.
The Gospel according to Mark, 73 C.E.
The Gospel according to Matthew, 80 C.E.
The Second Letter to the Thessalonians, 85 C.E.
The Gospel according to Luke, 90 C.E.
The Letter to the Ephesians, 90 C.E.
The Acts of the Apostles, 90 C.E.
The Epistle of James, 92 C.E.
The First Letter of Peter, 92 C.E.
The First Letter to Timothy, 93 C.E.
The Letter of Jude, 94 C.E.
The Epistle to the Hebrews, 95 C.E.
The Second Letter to Timothy, 96 C.E.
The Letter to Titus, 97 C.E.
The First Epistle of John, 98 C.E.
The Gospel according to John, 100 C.E.
The Second Epistle of John, 102 C.E.
The Third Epistle of John, 103 C.E.
Revelation, 105 C.E.
The Second Letter of Peter, 110 C.E.

In published Bibles these books appear in a different order, one that emerged as the result of agreement among churches during the fourth century:

The Gospel according to Matthew
The Gospel according to Mark
The Gospel according to Luke
The Gospel according to John
The Acts of the Apostles
The Letter to the Romans
The First Letter to the Corinthians
The Second Letter to the Corinthians
The Letter to the Galatians
The Letter to the Ephesians
The Letter to the Philippians
The Letter to the Colossians
The First Letter to the Thessalonians
The Second Letter to the Thessalonians
The First Letter to Timothy
The Second Letter to Timothy
The Letter to Titus
The Letter to Philemon
The Epistle to the Hebrews
The Epistle of James
The First Letter of Peter
The Second Letter of Peter
The First Epistle of John
The Second Epistle of John
The Third Epistle of John
The Letter of Jude
Revelation

Figure 1. Synagogue at Capernaum (visible remains from between the fourth and sixth centuries C.E.): Underneath the main hall the foundations of a first-century C.E. synagogue in black basalt have been uncovered. This is the location referred to in the story of Jesus' first exorcism in Mark 1:21-28. The building of the first-century synagogue is credited to a Roman centurion in Luke 7:5. *Photo by David Shankbone courtesy Wikimedia Commons (Creative Commons License 3.0).*

16

1

Jesus and his social worlds

The four Gospels in the New Testament, all written in the common Greek of the first century, reflect the cultures and concerns of the diverse Hellenistic cities that produced them. Their variety is fascinating, but the differences a reader finds as he or she moves from one Gospel to the next can cause confusion, and even frustration. What can we know about Jesus, when the Gospels do not fully agree, and sometimes contradict one another?

For example, only two Gospels narrate Jesus' birth. One account (Matthew 2.13–15) places Jesus and his family in Egypt just after his birth, while the other (Luke 2.22–38) insists they were in Jerusalem at that time. All four Gospels depict Jesus' crucifixion; yet they disagree in recording what his very last words were. Did he say, 'My God, my God, why have you forsaken me?' (Matthew 27.46; Mark 15.34) or, 'Father, into your hands I commend my spirit' (Luke 23.46) or, 'It is finished' (John 19.30)?

Attempts have been deployed over the centuries in a failed attempt to explain away such contradictions. But since the end of the eighteenth century scholars have shown – and people who have read all the Gospels through have generally agreed – that the Gospels are not verbatim histories of the events concerning Jesus. They are rather theological interpretations of his significance for believing communities, woven from memories about him.

This evaluation of the Gospels takes account of their religious purposes: they were designed to promote faith in Jesus, not to provide an objective account of his life. Whether the reader today approaches these texts as a believer or not, the fact of their religious origin needs to be acknowledged, if the Gospels are to be understood.

On any reading, the New Testament begins with Jesus, who is the origin of the faith that all the documents profess. Each Gospel reflects both the faith *of* Jesus, the beliefs he taught and lived and

17

died for, and faith *in* Jesus, the beliefs his followers made into a compelling religious movement.

The distinction between the faith of Jesus and faith in Jesus permits us to read the Gospels critically, with an eye to how we can distinguish his teaching and character from claims later made about him. Fortunately, there are powerful clues to his distinctive contribution within the Gospels. Although the Gospels were written in Greek, they refer to their Jesus as an Aramaic-speaking rabbi in Jewish Galilee, who took his message of 'the kingdom of God' throughout Israel, and then confronted the authorities in Jerusalem with such force that they had him crucified.

That journey involved Jesus in moving through differing cultural settings. The Mediterranean world of the first century, although linked by the widespread (but not universal) usage of Greek and by the powerful, often violent rule of the Roman empire, has been revealed by the modern study of history, anthropology, archaeology and language to be a place of deep diversity. The history of the formation of the Gospels themselves will concern us later, but from the outset we can say that the Gospels were composed through an evolutionary process that left traces of earlier cultural contexts beneath the surface of texts as they can be read today. Jesus moved through the cultural equivalent of microclimates during the course of his life, and sensitivity to the clues of the cultures reflected in the Gospels has permitted a much clearer picture of Jesus to emerge over the past generation of scholarship compared to previous centuries. For example, the language of a majority of Jews living in what had once been the nation-state of Israel was not Greek or even Hebrew, but Aramaic, the common language of the Near East since the time of the Persian Empire, and Aramaic is sometimes quoted verbatim in the Gospels.

Scholarly assessments of Jesus are hardly unanimous, and should not be expected to be, given the ferment of ideas surrounding him in current debate. There is nonetheless widespread agreement that five environments he negotiated prove crucial to understanding him. Those environments are (1) rural Jewish Galilee, (2) the movement of John the Baptist, (3) the towns Jesus encountered as a rabbi, (4) the rule of Herod Antipas, and (5) deep controversy concerning the Temple in Jerusalem. We cannot set out a full account of Jesus' life

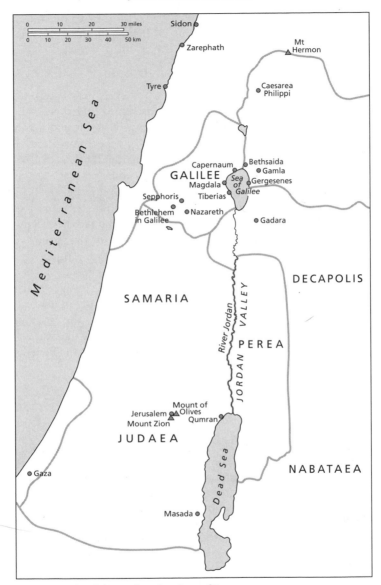

Map 1 Territorial Israel at the time of Jesus

here, but we can present five factors that need to be considered in any critical assessment of this rabbi and his significance.

Rural Jewish Galilee

Until recently, Jewish Galilee has been almost as mysterious as Jesus himself. Apart from the Gospels, in this regard and others, the writings of Josephus can be helpful. Josephus lived during the first century, taking part in the Jewish revolt against the Romans during 66–70 C.E.; he then defected and became a propagandist for his former enemies. Whatever one thinks of Josephus' integrity, he remains an invaluable resource for understanding the events, personalities and conditions of Israel at the time the New Testament emerged. Josephus describes Galilee as a proud region, resistant to the occupying force of Roman rule and its customs, valued for the fertility of its land and the quality of its produce.

Yet Josephus was a Judaean, a southerner, and a general who had tried and failed to master the proud Galilean people. Galilee in the north has lacked a voice of its own, because no written source, no body of Rabbinic literature, no scroll discovered in the midst of archaeological work, has been attributed to a Galilean of the first century. An oral culture, as resistant to change as it was to the Romans

---

Box 1.1. Josephus and Jesus

Flavius Josephus was born in Judaea in 37 C.E. and died about 100 C.E.. Although he was named Joseph at birth he took the name Flavius when he became a Roman citizen.

Near the beginning of the war against Rome (66–74 C.E.) Josephus led Galilean forces resisting Rome, but by 67, he had surrendered. Taken subsequently to Rome by the victorious Romans, he spent the rest of his life writing about the war (*Wars of the Jews*), about Judaean history and culture (*Antiquities*) and his own life (*Life*). He wrote in Greek for Jews and Gentile readers interested in Judaean culture. There are two passages about Jesus and one about John the Baptist.

Josephus' Testimony to Jesus (*Testimonium Flavianum*) is regarded as a significant extra-biblical reference to Jesus. Some scholars regard it as a forgery; most think it shows evidence of interpolations. Of the two versions given here, the first is in the Greek text while the second, shorter version is an Arabic version.

Antiquities 18.63–64:

> Now, there was about this time Jesus, a wise man, if indeed one ought to call him a man, for he was a doer of wonderful works – a teacher of such people as receive the truth with pleasure. He won over many of the Jews and many of the Greeks. He was [the] Christ; and when Pilate, at the suggestion of the principal men among us, had condemned him to the cross, those that loved him at the first did not forsake him, for he appeared to them alive again the third day, as the divine prophets had foretold these and ten thousand other wonderful things concern-ing him; and the tribe of Christians, so named from him, are not extinct at this day.

A tenth-century Arabic version occurs in Arabic in Agapius' *Book of the Title*, a history of the world from its beginning until 941/942 C.E.. Agapius was a tenth-century Christian Arab and Melkite bishop of Hierapolis. While this version is shorter and simpler, changes indicate that it is probably a paraphrase of an earlier account:

> At this time there was a wise man who was called Jesus, and his conduct was good, and he was known to be virtuous. And many people from among the Jews and the other nations became his disciples. Pilate condemned him to be crucified and to die. And those who had become his disciples did not abandon their loyalty to him. They reported that he had appeared to them three days after his crucifixion, and that he was alive. Accordingly they believed that he was the Messiah, concerning whom the Prophets have recounted wonders.

Josephus' second short reference to Jesus is an account of why Ananus was deposed as High Priest. Most scholars think Josephus identifies James as Jesus' brother (cf. Mark 6.3).

Antiquities 20.197–203:

And now Caesar, upon hearing the death of Festus, sent Albinus into Judaea, as procurator. But the king deprived Joseph of the high priesthood, and bestowed the succession to that office on the son of Ananus, who was also himself called Ananus. Now the report goes that this elder Ananus proved a most fortunate man; for he had five sons who had all performed the office of a high priest to God, and who had himself enjoyed that office a long time formerly, which had never happened to any other of our high priests. But this younger Ananus, who, as we have told you already, took the high priesthood, was a bold man in his temper, and very insolent; he was also of the sect of the Sadducees, who are very rigid in judging offenders, above all the rest of the Jews, as we have already observed; when, therefore, Ananus was of this disposition, he thought he had now a proper opportunity. Festus was now dead, and Albinus was but upon the road; so he assembled the Sanhedrin of judges, and brought before them the brother of Jesus, who was called Christ, whose name was James, and some others; and when he had formed an accusation against them as breakers of the law, he delivered them to be stoned: but as for those who seemed the most equitable of the citizens, and such as were the most uneasy at the breach of the laws, they disliked what was done; they also sent to King Agrippa, desiring him to send to Ananus that he should act so no more, for that what he had already done was not to be justified; some of them even went to meet Albinus, as he was upon his journey from Alexandria, and informed him that it was not lawful for Ananus to assemble the Sanhedrin without his consent. Whereupon Albinus complied with what they said, and wrote in anger to Ananus, and threatened that he would bring him to punishment for what he had done; on which king Agrippa took the high priesthood from him, when he had ruled but three months, and made Jesus, the son of Damnaeus, high priest.

who occupied it, Jewish Galilee condemned itself to silence from the point of view of history by its loyalty to the spoken word.

Archaeological excavation and study has greatly improved knowledge of Galilee as a result of work over the past twenty years. That new evidence underscores the isolation of rural Galilee from

Hellenistic culture, and attests the cultural integrity of Galilean Judaism. Tiny villages, hamlets for agriculture for the most part, persistently attest a great concern for purity, the definition of who exactly belongs to Israel and of how contact with those outside Israel should be regulated. Stone vessels for carrying water for purificatory washing are typically found. They are characteristic of Jewish villages, and quite unlike vessels for cooking or large cisterns used to store water for drinking, which are common throughout the Near East. Stone vessels for purification are more persistent in Galilee than the *miqveh*, the stepped bathing pool, or the synagogue, but all of these have been found, and they lead to a single, clear conclusion. Jewish Galilee had established institutions and practices that put it outside any supposed assimilation within Graeco-Roman culture.

All these finds have shattered the myth of a purely Hellenistic Jesus living in a thoroughly Romanized Galilee. Until a synagogue was found in Galilean Gamla, it was routinely claimed that synagogues were only a post-Christian institution. Before *miqvaoth* were discovered in several towns, bathing was often dismissed as purely the elitist practice of Pharisees in Judaea (for more on Pharisees see the box on p. 41). Indeed, it was even said that Jesus spoke Greek, rather than Aramaic, despite the fact that actual transliterations of Aramaic appear in the Greek Gospels. Now the discovery of the Dead Sea Scrolls shows that Aramaic was widely used during the first century and earlier, and the discovery of non-sectarian scrolls near Qumran, a carefully designed settlement of Essenes on the shores of the Dead Sea, shows the wide usage of Aramaic.

The archaeological Galilee is a Jewish Galilee, as far as Jesus and his movement are concerned; garrison enclaves such as Sepphoris, although near to Nazareth, are notable for their absence from Jesus' itinerary in the Gospels. Nazareth itself was a tiny settlement of no more than a couple of hundred people, who lived in earthen sheds around courtyards for common cooking and milling, with a central facility for pressing wine and olives. The archaeological and textual scholarship of the past two decades has revolutionized how we should think about Galilee and about Judaism, and that means the once fashionable (and in some circles, still fashionable) picture of Jesus as an Athenian in Jewish dress must change.

Box 1.2. The Dead Sea Scrolls

The Dead Sea Scrolls are a collection of 900 fragmentary scrolls discovered between 1947 and 1956 in eleven caves in the cliffs along the left bank of the Dead Sea. Until this find, there was no Jewish text in Hebrew or Aramaic that could be definitely dated to the first century c.e.. Texts date from 150 b.c.e. to 70 c.e.. The find includes versions of biblical texts, biblical commentaries, parabiblical writings like the *Genesis Apocryphon*, community regulations, liturgical works and apocalyptic visions. Manuscripts are identified by cave number, Q, and the manuscript number or an abbreviated title. 11QTemple is the *Temple Scroll* from cave eleven. Scholars who first studied the scrolls identified them as the library of the Jewish sect of the Essenes based in the adjacent settlement at Qumran.

Jewish Galilee was a peasant culture, grounded in an economy of exchange and occasional trade. For the great majority of families living there, keeping to themselves away from centers of Roman power, maintaining Israelite identity was not a matter of formal learning, because most people were illiterate, but of oral memory, local custom and occasional pilgrimage to Jerusalem. Above all, that identity was guaranteed by the common knowledge within a given community of each person's mother and father. In later Judaism, having a Jewish mother was enough to make one an Israelite. During the first century, however, not knowing who a person's father was made him a *mamzer*.

At base, a *mamzer* was the product of a union that was forbidden, because the couple were not permitted to marry and procreate according to the Torah, the Law of Moses, which set out severe punishments for illicit sexual contact. The Mishnah, a manual of Rabbinic rulings from the time both before and after Jesus, clearly sets out this definition (see Mishnah *Qiddushin* 3.12). Whatever became of the man and the woman as the result of their relationship, their offspring was considered an Israelite, but an irregular Israelite.

The same judgment applied in the Mishnah (*Ketubbot* 1.9) to a case such as Jesus': the offspring of a woman whose sexual partner was not known with certainty. If the community in which a person lived did not know who that person's father was, for example because his parents were not living together, that made the person a *mamzer*. In later Judaism, this severe standard changed. According to the Talmud, which was composed centuries later than the Mishnah, a person is a *mamzer* only if it was known that his or her father was a Gentile (*Qiddushin* 70a). But that is a later standard, which reflects the adjustment of Jewish law to the circumstances produced by two defeats at the hands of the Romans (with rapes and forced 'marriages' on a massive scale). During the first century, as the Mishnah indicates, the more stringent standard applied, and that had a profound impact on Jesus.

Deuteronomy 23.2 specifies that a *mamzer* is to be excluded from the congregation until the *tenth generation* after him, a severe penalty that permanently marginalized a person of that status and his progeny. Understandably, the term was applied with caution, and its application was subject to debate and change. The precise description of Mary's pregnancy in Matthew 1.18, as occurring between the time a contract of marriage was exchanged and the actual cohabitation of the couple, put Jesus into the position of being considered a *mamzer* within first-century practice.

As a result of these circumstances, some people accused Jesus of being born of fornication (*porneia*, John 8.41). Others, from his own town (Mark 6.3), called him 'son of Mary' rather than 'son of Joseph', although some of his followers proudly identified him as Joseph's son (John 1.45), and that was one root of the title 'son of David' as applied to Jesus. The story of Jesus' miraculous birth, one of several explanations of his paternity in the New Testament, addresses the same situation. Whoever Jesus' natural father was – Joseph prior to his actual residence with Mary, another man to whom Mary was not married while Joseph was her betrothed, or the power of the most high (Luke 1.35) – Jesus was a *mamzer* within the terms of reference of first-century Judaism. This category provoked the disparate views of Jesus' birth attested in the New Testament and, to a lesser extent, in Rabbinic literature as well.

The movement of John the Baptist

John the Baptist is a crucial figure in Jesus' development, and not only because he personally baptized Jesus. John also contributed two related – and signally important – themes to what Jesus taught and did.

Josephus shows how prominent John was within his time, emphasizing John's popularity and political influence (Josephus,

---

Box 1.3. Josephus and John the Baptist

Josephus' account of John the Baptist (*Antiquities* 18.109–19) is thought by most scholars to be basically historical. It occurs in an account regarding Herod Antipas, tetrarch of Galilee and son of Herod the Great.

About this time Aretas, the king of Petra, and Herod the Tetrarch had a quarrel on account of the following. Herod the tetrarch had married the daughter of Aretas and had lived with her a great while; but once when he was on his way to Rome he lodged with his half-brother, also named Herod but who had a different mother, the high priest Simon's daughter. There he fell in love with Herodias, this latter Herod's wife, who was the daughter of their brother Aristobulus and the sister of Agrippa the Great.

This man ventured to talk to her about a marriage between them; she accepted, and an agreement was made for her to come to him as soon as he should return from Rome, one condition of this marriage being that he should divorce Aretas' daughter. So when he had made this agreement, he sailed to Rome; but when he had finished there and returned again, his wife, having discovered the agreement he had made with Herodias, and before he knew that she knew of the plan, asked him to send her to Machaerus, a place on the border between the territories of Aretas and Herod, without informing him of any of her intentions.

Accordingly Herod sent her there, thinking his wife had not perceived anything. But she had sent messages a good while before to Machaerus, which had been under the control of her father, and so all things necessary for her escape were made ready for her by the general of Aretas' army. By that means

---

she soon came into Arabia, under the conduct of the several generals, who carried her from one to another successively; and soon she came to her father and told him of Herod's intentions.

Aretas made this the start of his enmity toward Herod. He also had a quarrel with him about their boundaries in the area of Gabalis. So they raised armies on both sides and prepared for war, sending their generals to fight instead of themselves. And when they had joined battle, all Herod's army was destroyed by the treachery of some fugitives who, though they were of the tetrarchy of Philip and joined the army, betrayed him. So Herod wrote about these affairs to Emperor Tiberius, who was very angry at the attempt made by Aretas and wrote to Vitellius to make war upon him and either to take him alive, and bring him in chains, or to kill him, and send him his head. This was the command that Tiberius gave to the governor of Syria.

Now some of the Jews thought that the destruction of Herod's army came from God, and was a very just punishment for what he did against John called the baptist. For Herod had him killed, although he was a good man and had urged the Jews to exert themselves to virtue, both as to justice toward one another and reverence toward God, and having done so join together in washing. For immersion in water, it was clear to him, could not be used for the forgiveness of sins, but as a sanctification of the body, and only if the soul was already thoroughly purified by right actions. And when others massed about him, for they were very greatly moved by his words, Herod, who feared that such strong influence over the people might carry to a revolt – for they seemed ready to do any thing he should advise – believed it much better to move now than later have it raise a rebellion and engage him in actions he would regret.

And so John, out of Herod's suspiciousness, was sent in chains to Machaerus, the fort previously mentioned, and there put to death; but it was the opinion of the Jews that out of retribution for John God willed the destruction of the army so as to afflict Herod.

Both Josephus and the Gospels agree that Herod Antipas had John killed but for different reasons. Thus Josephus and the Gospels present alternative accounts of the same figure.

Antiquities 18.106–19). Josephus also confirms a basic element of the presentation of the Gospels: John expected Israelites to purify themselves by confessing their sins and receiving forgiveness while immersing in water, and he believed that God's Spirit would one day be bestowed on those who engaged in the preparation he demanded.

Immersion, for John, was not a once-for-all act, as it later became in Christian baptism. In the practice of the early Church, believers felt that they received the Spirit of God when they were immersed in the name of Jesus. That conviction emerged *after* the resurrection, and stemmed from the belief that Jesus was alive at the right hand of God, and able to dispense divine Spirit (see Acts 2.33). But in John's practice, as in Judaism as a whole, purification was a routine requirement, and people could return to John many times. They naturally engaged in many forms of purification other than John's, whether in their villages or at the Temple. Impurity was a fact of life, as routine as childbirth and preparing a loved one's body for burial, for example, and therefore so was purification.

John offered purification within the usual understanding of Judaism, but he did so in the wilderness, teaching that natural-gathered (or 'living') water supplied by God made people ready for worship and access to the Temple, provided that immersion was accompanied by repentance. Within John's activity, there was also an esoteric meaning. John conveyed a definite understanding of the final significance that his purification for Israel offered.

As John himself expressed it, immersing oneself in water prepared one to receive the Spirit of God himself, which was to drench all Israel with its sanctification. The key to John's idea of immersion being a preparation for God himself lies in the wording attributed to him, 'I immerse you in water, but he himself will immerse you in Holy Spirit' (Mark 1.8; see Matthew 3.11; Luke 3.16). Within the context of Christianity after the resurrection, those words are ful-filled when the risen Jesus endows believers with God's Spirit (again, see Acts 2.33). Within the context of John the Baptist long before the death and resurrection of Jesus, however, what is at issue was the purification that prepares the way for God to give his own Spirit in the future.

To make his way to John, Jesus had to depart from Galilee, and live in the Judaean wilderness, where John was active. John's two concerns, purity and the Spirit of God, focused on the place on earth where in early Judaism purity and forgiveness were most celebrated and God's Spirit was universally recognized: the Temple in Jerusalem. Jesus did not simply meet his teacher after he became an adult (as a superficial reading of the Gospels, as if they were literal history, would suggest), but apprenticed himself to John as a youth.

Josephus indicates that John the Baptist was executed by Herod Antipas in 21 c.e. (*Antiquities* 18.109–19); Jesus must have associated himself with John long before John's death to have thoroughly assimilated his master's teaching. What Josephus does not say, but the Gospels do attest (Mark 6.18–29; Matthew 14.3–12; Luke 3.19–20; 9.9), is that John criticized Antipas for breaking the Torah by marrying Herodias, who had previously been married to Antipas' brother. As a teacher of purity, John naturally attacked this action, because it broke the Law of Moses (Leviticus 20.21). Antipas reacted to this challenge to the legitimacy of his marriage by having John arrested and executed. Josephus' account dovetails with the Gospels, and shows how the New Testament is best read within the context of the literature of its time.

Jesus' extensive period of study and even controversy with John, indicated by John's Gospel (John 3.22–36), allows time for Jesus to remain in the land of Judaea *and to practise immersion himself,* as John 3.22 specifically states he did. Although this Gospel then tries to take its assertion back (John 4.1–3), the initial statement is emphatic, unambiguous and in all probability historical: Jesus practised a ministry of immersion comparable to John's.

The Synoptic Gospels are quite plain about when Jesus' characteristic, public ministry began: as Mark 1.14 puts it, 'after John was delivered over' (see the comparable formulations of Matthew 4.12; Luke 3.19–20). From the point of view of Herod Antipas, Jesus represented no immediate continuation of John's threat, because Jesus had stopped immersing Israelites as John had been doing. When Herod later *did* react to Jesus with the threat of violence (Mark 6.14–16; Matthew 14.1–2; Luke 9.7–9), the issue was his activity of healing, not baptism.

Even as Jesus desisted from John's practice of immersion, he intensified John's second focus: awareness of God's Spirit. This signature concern of John's activity, which also became a hallmark of Jesus' emphasis, took up a theme from the book of Ezekiel (Ezekiel 36.25–27). The close and causal connection between water and Spirit there is the precedent for John's baptism, and his prophecy that Israel was going to enjoy a new accessibility of God's presence.

Ezekiel was also the central text of Jewish mysticism, the practice of God's presence, visualized as centred on his movable throne, the chariot or *Merkavah* (in Aramaic). Traces of this *Merkavah* mysticism are plain in the story of Jesus' baptism.

John practised a personal discipline (or *kabbalah* in Aramaic) of envisioning the Throne of God, the spiritual counterpart of his practice of immersion, which made it possible for John to speak of baptism in the Spirit. He and his disciples saw the Spirit of God before the *Merkavah*, ready to drench Israel, just as Israel was drenched in the waters of purification. Careful discipline, repetitive, committed practice, and sometimes-inadequate diet and exposure to the elements all contributed to the vividness of visions of God's throne, and visionary narratives are a significant aspect of the literature of the New Testament.

The Gospels all relate the baptism of Jesus in a way that foreshadows baptism in early Christianity. But they also refer to the particular vision of Jesus, which not every baptized Christian could or did claim (Mark 1.9–11; cf. Matthew 3.13–17; Luke 3.21–22). As Jesus was immersed for purification, following John's teaching, he came to have an increasingly vivid vision, of the heavens splitting open, and God's Spirit coming upon him. And a voice: 'You are my son, beloved; in you I take pleasure.'

Each of these elements is resonant with the Israelite mysticism of the divine throne. The heavens are viewed as multiple, hard shells above the earth, so that any real disclosure of the divine must represent a rending of those firmaments. But once opened, Jesus' vision is not of ascending through the heavens, as in *1 Enoch* (from the Pseudepigrapha), but of the Spirit, as a dove, hovering over him and descending. That image is a vivid realization that the Spirit of God at creation once hovered over the face of the primeval waters (Genesis 1.2), as a bird. The bird was identified as a dove in Rabbinic tradition, and a fragment from Qumran supports the association. The Spirit, which would one day come to Israel, in Jesus' vision was already upon him, and God took pleasure in him as a 'son'.

Jesus' approach to the *Merkavah* by means of John's teaching had opened the prospect that the gates of heaven were open again for the Spirit to descend upon Israel and pour outward to the nations. Jesus' conscious framing of a personal tradition or *kabbalah*, an approach to the divine *Merkavah* for himself and for his disciples, naturally included an understanding of his own identity. Clearly, the association of Jesus as God's son gained currency as a consequence of the resurrection. But its currency is very difficult to explain, if Jesus himself avoided this designation. *Some* consistent usage of messianic language would likely have been in the background of Jesus' teaching for the term to emerge as the primary designation of Jesus. Anointed by the Spirit of God, Jesus viewed himself as enacting and articulating the claims of God's transforming power ('the kingdom of God'). Once Jesus' approach to the *Merkavah*, on the basis of his endowment with Spirit, is seen to be the pivot of his experience and his program of activity, his care in defining how he was God's son acquires its sense. He said God's Spirit was upon him, and anointed him (Luke 4.18), so that he could make God known as his son: 'Everything has been delivered over to me by my father' (Luke 10.32).

The towns Jesus encountered as a rabbi

Jesus returned to his native Galilee after the death of John the Baptist, and that was when he took up his characteristic message of 'the kingdom of God'. He taught as a rabbi, but he also called attention, in the manner of the prophets, to how God was transforming the world, as the king of all creation. In common with the greatest prophets of his region centuries before, Elijah and Elisha, Jesus was reputed to be endowed with miraculous powers. Like them, he could render people who were impure owing to skin disease pure again (see 2 Kings 5 and Mark 1.40–45), heal even those thought

31

to be dead (see 1 Kings 17.17–24 and Mark 5.35–42), and invoke signs of God's presence such as feeding many people with little food (see 2 Kings 4.42–44 and Mark 6.30–44). The last similarity is relevant, because Jesus used the imagery of feasting in order to refer to the kingdom of God, the alternative to human rule that he believed was transforming the world. As in the cases of prophets before his time, the belief that God confirmed Jesus' teaching by means of miracles is a matter of historical record, however one might explain miraculous events.

The picture of God offering a feast on Mount Zion 'for all peoples', where death itself is swallowed up, had been current from the time of Isaiah 25.6–8. In synagogue worship, the congregation heard the Scriptures recited in what became their language for centuries, Aramaic. This Aramaic recitation was called a 'Targum', the Aramaic word for 'translation', but in fact some Targums include new wording as compared to Hebrew originals, and reflect the creative religious language of ancient Judaism. The Targum of Isaiah refers to the divine disclosure on Mount Zion with the verbatim phrase 'the kingdom of the Lord of hosts' (24.23). Jesus' practice of fellowship at meals with his disciples and many others amounted to a claim that the ultimate festivity God desired had already begun. He even promised a prophetic feast with the patriarchs of Israel, raised from the dead, when his followers would recline like aristocrats on couches (Matthew 8.11; Luke 13.29).

Apart from its vivid imagery, the economics of this assertion are striking. Wealth that a Galilean could scarcely imagine is to be enjoyed in the most fundamental medium of peasant exchange – the festive communal meal. This statement is a surreal promise in the context of Nazareth (as in the context of Galilee as a whole); in the setting of the periodic movements of rebellion that broke out in this region, such an economic transformation must have carried with it in the minds of some practitioners at least an implication that foreign wealth was to be appropriated.

In contrast to his embrace of wealth within festal imagery, Jesus also, in a prophetic manner, attacked the wealth that leads to oppression, during the period of his settled activity as a rabbi in Capernaum, a fishing town that he deliberately made his dwelling place in Galilee (Matthew 4.13–16). Despite living there with

Simon and Andrew, moreover, he also voiced the prophetic demand for conventions of wealth to melt away (Luke 6.20b–23):

> The poor are favoured, because *yours* is the kingdom of God; Those who hunger now are favoured, because you will be satisfied; Those who weep now are favoured, because you will laugh; You are favoured, when humanity hates you and when they exclude you and censure you and put out your name as evil on the one like the person's account. Rejoice in that day and skip, for look: your reward is great in the heaven; for their fathers did the same things to the prophets.

At first, it seems odd to find these words attributed to Jesus during his period in Capernaum. After all, here was a Jewish town – of a thousand or two rather than a few hundred – with a synagogue and genuine comfort: distinctive houses of basalt, with windows, stairs to upper storeys, ornamental pebbles on the floors, and the relatively luxurious furnishings of ceramic lamps, plates, bowls and cups. All quite unlike Nazareth, and potentially an image of just the sort of festivity Jesus had spoken of in the hill country of Galilee. And yet what had been praised as a metaphor is rejected when it becomes reality.

Confronted with wealth, he praises poverty, or so it might seem at first. But the situation is actually more complex. Capernaum lived off its well-developed port and fishing industry – a coordinated commerce involving those who caught fish, those who stored, those who salted and those who sold. Commerce that complex necessarily involved currency. From the year 19/20 c.e. Herod Antipas had coins struck for towns such as Capernaum at nearby Tiberius. Josephus attests the existence of landless Galileans during this period, who were attracted not only to established towns such as Capernaum, but to the newly founded Tiberias, whose construction on an old cemetery enraged local sentiment against it, but made for cheap land, and even free homesteads donated by Herod Antipas (*Antiquities* 18.36–8).

Jesus' well-known imperative to the townspeople of Capernaum is to reverse this progression, to give away property and follow him along with the other disciples (Mark 10.17–31, cf. the analogous passages in Matthew 19.16–30 and Luke 18.18–30). The urgency of this imperative is especially plain in v. 25, 'It is easier for a camel to go through the eye of a needle than for a rich person to enter into the kingdom of God.' A policy of disposing of wealth in order to alleviate poverty is evident both here and elsewhere in the traditions of the New Testament, along with a claim that the reversion to an exchange economy by means of wealth so disposed will bring eternal rewards.

Within the actual conditions of Capernaum, of course, there was virtually no chance that such a policy could succeed among the general population. It is no coincidence that it is precisely to that town that Jesus says (Luke 10.15; cf. Matthew 11.23): 'And you, Capernaum, will you be exalted to heaven? No, you will be brought down to Hades.'

Nonetheless, Capernaum, rather than Nazareth, became the center of Jesus' activity, owing to the hospitality and the following he enjoyed there. Two pairs of brothers, Peter and Andrew, James and John, stand out as leaders – and leading supporters, from their family holdings in Capernaum – of Jesus' movement at this stage, from around 24 C.E. (Matthew 4.18–22; Mark 1.16–20). They commanded sufficient resources to be able to support Jesus as well as their own families, and yet kept a sufficient distance from the economic system of the Roman estates so as to enable Jesus to persist in his criticism of unjust *mammon*, as he said in Aramaic (Luke 16.1–9). This period saw Jesus taken into the home of Peter, and his growing reputation as a healer (Matthew 4.23–25; 8.14–15; Mark 1.29–39; Luke 4.38–44). He had been known as a visitor to the synagogue who exorcized unclean spirits (Mark 1.21–28; Luke 4.31–37), but his actual residence there caused a genuine following to gather around him. He became not only a charismatic rabbi, but the conscious leader of a movement designed to promulgate the kingdom of God. Indeed, journeys outward from Capernaum were to some extent undertaken, the Synoptic Gospels indicate, to avoid the crush of casual sympathizers (Mark 1.35–38; Luke 4.42–43).

Small villages in Galilee became as characteristic of Jesus' activity as streams in the Jordan Valley were within John's. In political terms, the villages provided camouflage for Jesus. They were not wilderness, and nothing to do with the Jordan Valley, the place of John's opposition to Herod Antipas. But they were also quite unlike a city (particularly Sepphoris, a garrison and seat of Antipas' power), where Herod's official presence as well as the occupying Romans were forces to be reckoned with.

The rule of Herod Antipas

Despite his avoidance of cities and his different pattern of activity from John's, Jesus came to Antipas' attention (Luke 13.31–33):

> In that hour some Pharisees came forward, saying to him, 'Get out and go from here! Because Herod wants to kill you.' And he said to them, 'You go, and say to that fox, "Look, I put out demons and will send healings today and tomorrow, and on the third day I will be completed." Except that I must go today and tomorrow and the following day, because it is not acceptable that a prophet should perish outside of Jerusalem!'

Jesus puts himself into the general category of prophets who will be killed as a result of their prophecy and sets out to avoid Herod Antipas (see Figure 1 overleaf). When final confrontation with authorities would take place, that was to be in Jerusalem, in the manner of several prophets before Jesus.

Jesus' exorcisms and healings – his reputation as a wonder worker after the model of Elijah and Elisha – had come to Antipas' attention, and Antipas also knew of Jesus' connection to John the Baptist (Mark 6.14–16; Matthew 14.1–2; Luke 9.7–9). By the year 27 C.E. or during the 'fifteenth year of Tiberius' (Luke 3.1, the only chronological notice in the Gospels of Jesus' public activity), Jesus had become too well known to continue to make Capernaum his permanent base.

The support of his disciples now became crucial to Jesus. To them he entrusted his most treasured possession: the teaching he had crafted in order to convey his sense of how God was in the process of transforming the world. His emblematic approach to God in the Lord's Prayer was central to that instruction. The names of the disciples vary in the New Testament somewhat (see Matthew 10.2–4; Mark 3.16–19; Luke 6.13–16; Acts 1.13) for two main reasons. First, there was a confusion between the large group who followed Jesus around Galilee to learn his teaching as thoroughly

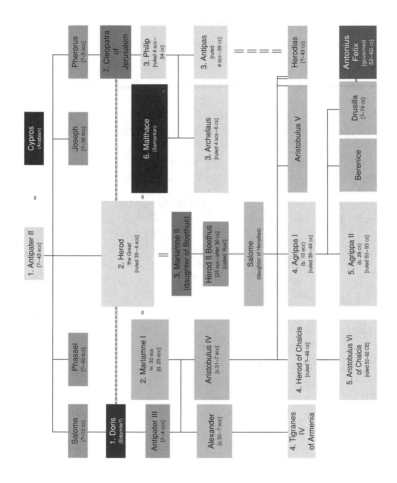

Key		
Ruler – client of Rome		Lesser heir of Hasmonean priests
Lesser descendant		Non-Hasmonean Jewish spouse
Roman procurator		Non-Jewish spouse
= double line > married		single line > descendants
1. order of succession		1. order of Herod's marriages

NOTE

Herod's wives create logistical problems for graphic representation of all his descendants and their complex inter-relationships. The five wives presented above (indicated by a double line: ==) are those whose children had the greatest impact on the history of the House of Herod. For completeness, however, the following table lists all of Herod's ten wives and 16 children. Since Josephus (Antiquities 17.19–22) does not give details on most of the marriages and births but, instead, claims that Herod practised polygamy like the Hebrew patriarchs, the numbering in this table should not be interpreted as an exact historical sequence.

Wife	Son(s)	Daughter(s)	
1. Doris	1. Antipater III		
2. Mariamne	2. Alexander	4. Salampsio*	
	3. Aristobulus IV	5. Cypros II	
3. Mariamne II	6. Herod II	7. Salome	
		8. Phaesalis	
4. ? (daughter of his sister, Salome)	(none)	(none)	
5. ? (daughter of his brother, Pheroras)	(none)	(none)	
6. Malthace	9. Archelaus	11. Olympias	
	10. Antipas		
7. Cleopatra of Jerusalem	12. Philip		
	13. Herod		
8. Pallas	14. Phaesalus	15. Roxanne	
9. Phedra		16. Salome	
10. Elpis			

* Herod's oldest daughter Salampsio (4) was married to Phasael II, the son of Herod's older brother by the same name. They had three sons and two daughters, the youngest of whom (Cypros III, named after Herod's mother) was married to her cousin Agrippa I, the son of her mother's brother, Aristobulus IV (3). She was the mother of Agrippa II. (Marrying daughters to uncles or cousins was common in the family of Herod and other contemporary rulers and was not regarded by Romans or Jews as incest.)

Reference: Josephus, Antiquities 17.19–22.

Figure 2 The house of Herod

Box 1.4. Pray then like this...

The prayer that Jesus taught his disciples has become known as the Lord's Prayer and is found in two places in the Gospels, Matthew 6.9–15 and Luke 11.1–4. A third version of the prayer is also found in the *Didache*, an early non-canonical text (for this text see p. 51).

The three versions are not exactly the same, and it is likely that oral variations account for the differences. Despite the differences each version has two parts: the first addresses God and the second makes requests of God for food, forgiveness of debts and deliverance from temptation and evil.

The opening address to God is consonant with the theology of the particular text in which it appears (for more on the work of the Gospel writers in crafting their narrative see pp. 104–17). Luke's version of the Lord's Prayer opens with the direct address of Jesus to God, 'Father, hallowed be your name.' Matthew emphasizes the location of the heavenly Father: 'Our father, the one in the heavens', which is consistent with his instruction to 'call no one father on earth for you have one father, the one in the heavens' (23.9). In Matthew, Jesus instructs the disciples to pray succinctly within the wider context of the Sermon on the Mount (Matthew 5–7), an epitome, or summary, of Jesus' message.

Only the *Didache*'s version of the Lord's Prayer concludes with a doxology, that is, a concluding ascription of glory to God. Texts show that various doxologies were added to the Matthaean and Lucan versions of the Lord's Prayer as its liturgical use developed.

At the heart of the Lord's Prayer is the request that God's name be known and God's reign actualized. These ideas echo prayers and narratives of Hebrew Scriptures. Exodus 3.14, for example, records the revelation of God's name; Psalm 145 celebrates God's name and the spread of God's kingdom. Only when God's kingdom comes fully will God be honoured and glorified (Ezekiel 36.20–23). Jewish prayers that may have been in use in the first century C.E., such as parts of the Eighteen Benedictions (or *Tefillah*, literally 'prayer'), ask for forgiveness for the sake of God's name. According to Mishnah *Berakhot* 4.1, the *Tefillah* was said three times daily, as was the Lord's Prayer, according to the *Didache* 8.2–3.

as they could, and the select twelve whom at a later stage Jesus delegated to speak and act on his behalf (Matthew 10.1; Mark 6.7; Luke 9.1).

Luke expands the select group to include 70 or 72 people (Luke 10.1), but that is a symbolic number, corresponding to the traditional number in Judaism of all the non-Jewish nations of the world; Luke's Gospel manifests a particular interest in the promise of Jesus for the Gentiles. The 70 could also represent the 70 elders chosen by Moses in Numbers 11.24–25, but Luke's interests make that less likely. A reasonable estimate is that twenty or thirty disciples in the vicinity of Capernaum, some with wives and children, followed Jesus as best they could. But of course, not all of them could follow him all the time, and the identity of the group would change. That brings us to the second reason for the variation of the names: the larger group of his disciples, from whom the delegates were chosen, came and went, some defecting because they came to disagree with Jesus' increasingly radical teaching.

One element of controversy was Jesus' acceptance of the fellowship of a woman described as sinful (Luke 7.36–50). Female disciples are named, including Mary Magdalene, whom Jesus exorcized repeatedly (8.1–3). The element of scandal here is probably not discussion with women, which was permitted even later in Rabbinic circles, but travel with them, which could not help but prompt suspicions of impropriety. When Jesus spoke of a woman baking as an instance of divine kingdom (Luke 13.21) or referred to himself as a mother bird gathering her young (Matthew 23.37), he was not just inventing arresting images. The lush fecundity of Wisdom, an emphatically feminine image of divine power (see Proverbs 8.22–31), was as basic to God as sexuality was to the people created in God's image, and in one case Jesus even spoke in Wisdom's name (Luke 11.49).

Jesus acknowledged defections from his own controversial views in his parables. The parable of the sower and its interpretation (Mark 4.1–9, 13–20; Matthew 13.1–9, 18–23; Luke 8.4–8, 11–15) expressly involves a theology of failure, the recognition that the word of the kingdom would not always prove productive after sowing. He could even speak trenchantly of someone who sowed bad seed in the midst of good (Matthew 13.24–30), and of fish caught, only to be destroyed

(Matthew 13.47–50). These are parables of harsh judgment, directed against those once associated with Jesus, who had proved themselves useless, or even as hostile.

Opposition was inevitable, from many ordinary practitioners of Judaism, including the Pharisees. In a Rabbinic fashion, Jesus applied Pharisaic principles to respond to their objections. His stance sometimes reflected teachings in the Mishnah. A rabbi named Hillel (50 B.C.E.–10 C.E.) had argued that the inside of a vessel, whether pure or impure, determined the purity or impurity of the whole vessel

Box 1.5. Parables

Parables lie at the heart of Jesus' proclamation of God's realm. Much research on the parables attempts to uncover information about the historical Jesus and his teaching or the intentions of Gospel writers. Other approaches stress reader-oriented interpretations focused away from historical context and towards readers as co-creators of meaning.

Parables are considered as metaphors from a common stock of proverbial comparisons. (In fact, the term translated from Hebrew into English as 'parable' most basically means 'comparison'.) Thus in the parable of the Prodigal Son, Jesus uses a theme from Israelite traditions in which the younger son succeeded at the expense of the elder (compare Cain and Abel; Jacob and Esau). The parable can be read and renamed as a story of restored harmony between estranged children and forgiving fathers. A socio-critical interpretation reads the parable as a Mediterranean family story about a dysfunctional relationship between a father and two sons in which the younger son behaves inappropriately in asking for his inheritance before the father has died. A reader interested in feminist concerns might ask the whereabouts of the mother or sisters in the parable. We might also ask why the younger son has run away in the first place. If, for example, an implied reader with a history of sexual abuse reads the parable, the return of the prodigal son to the patriarchal family could be unhelpful for abused victims. The point here is to recognize that the experi-ence of a reader affects interpretation of the text.

(in the Mishnah, see *Kelim* 25.6). In his criticism of the Pharisees, Jesus adhered to Hillel's principle: cleanness proceeds from within to without and purifies the whole. But if that is the case with cups, he argued with a flash of insight that disarmed his opponents, then all the more so with Israelites who are pure by their intention and the way they work the land. It is what is *within* that makes a person pure. His well-known aphorism conveys just this insight: it is not what goes into a person that defiles one, but what comes out of a person defiles one (Mark 7.15; see also Matthew 15.11). Against the Pharisees, Jesus asserted that purity was a matter of the totality of one's being. One was either clean or unclean; for Jesus, there was no vacillation. The Pharisees' policy for dealing with specific, exterior sources of defilement, skilfully crafted to deal with the complexities of urban pluralism, found no resonance in his mind, formed by the relative isolation of rural Galilee.

The threat of Antipas accounts for Jesus' crossing into Herod Philip's territory (at first in Bethsaida, where some of his disciples had relatives) east of the Sea of Galilee. In stark contrast with Jesus'

Box 1.6. Pharisees

Josephus claims to have been a Pharisee (*Life* 9–12) and Paul is associated with them by his own testimony (Philippians 3.4–6). Josephus describes them as a philosophical sect, attributing to them a belief in an imperishable soul, and eternal punishment for the souls of the wicked. They believe in fate, free will, and God. They make no concession to luxury, and show respect for their elders. In the Gospels the Pharisees often debate with Jesus about issues of purity, including Sabbath observance, fasting, and tithing. The dispute between Jesus and the Pharisees about eating with unclean hands enables Gospel writers to distinguish the Pharisees' 'traditions of the elders' from the commandments of God (Mark 7.1–23; Matthew 15.1–20). The Pharisees may have been a lay group concerned with interpretation and application of religious piety to everyday life, especially as they were concerned with maintaining a standard of purity consistent with worship in the Temple.

acceptance – albeit at a safe distance from the danger Capernaum now posed – of the delegation from the centurion garrisoned there (Matthew 8.5–13; Luke 7.1–10), his reaction to an attempt at reconciliation by his own family was forbidding (Mark 3.31–35; Matthew 12.46–50; Luke 8.19–21). When they sent a delegation of family friends to him, he would not interrupt his teaching to greet them: 'Whoever does the will of God that is my brother and sister and mother.' Still more surprising is his sojourn in Decapolis. Despite some success (Mark 7.31–37; Matthew 15.29–31), the time in Decapolis proved a disaster on the whole, in that Jesus' practice of purity and the proudly Hellenistic ethos of that region were as incompatible as the pure waters of the sea of Galilee proved to be with the swine that drowned therein (Mark 5.1–20; Matthew 8.28–34; Luke 8.26–39).

The fiasco of attempting to establish a base outside territorial Israel led Jesus to the innovation of the Twelve, a number that relates to the theological purpose of the institution. Hunted by Herod Antipas in Galilee itself, uncertain of safety within the domain of Herod Philip, repulsed by the Gentile population east of the Sea of Galilee, where exactly could Jesus go? How could he continue to reach Galilee with his message?

His response to this dilemma was a stroke of genius that assured the wider promulgation of the message of the kingdom: he dispatched twelve disciples as delegates on his behalf. The practice of sending a delegate (a *shaliach*) was common in the Middle East to seal a marriage or business contract. The role of 'apostle', from the Greek term *apostolos* (which translates *shaliach*) came out of the ordinary practice of sending a go-between to settle routine transactions. Jesus applied this custom of personal, business and military life to spread his own ideas and practices. He dispatched each *shaliach* to do what he did: proclaim God's kingdom and heal (Matthew 10.1–16; Mark 6.6–13; Luke 9.1–5).

Those who were sent by Jesus had crossed with him into Herod Philip's territory. There was Peter, his 'Rock', the two noisy brothers James and John, Andrew, Philip, Bartholomew, Matthew, Thomas, another James (son of Alphaeus), Thaddaeus, Simon called 'Zealot', and Judas Iscariot (Mark 3.16–18; Matthew 10.2–4; Luke 6.14–16). Other disciples, such as Nathanael and Kleopas, did not take on the role of a delegate, which involved more hardship than honor; it is not surprising that only twelve (rather than the 70 of Luke) took on the task.

Yet their success was such that Jesus could not avoid confronting the possibility of militant insurrection, as is reflected in the feeding of the five thousand (John 6.1–15; Mark 6.32–44; Matthew 14.13–21; Luke 9.10–17). The Gospels (but for Luke, which places the incident near Bethsaida) report that five thousand men followed Jesus into the Syrian wilderness, but the precise number obviously cannot be known. The total population of Galilee was about 150,000 at this point, less than half of whom were Jews living among the 204 cities and villages (Josephus, *Life* 235); even one thousand would have represented some 4 per cent of able-bodied Jewish men, the most militant arm of Galilean Judaism. Jesus' movement had become politically significant, but militarily far short of overwhelming. Over a period of several months, what have been described as would-be zealots abandoned their families, left their peasant life behind and their hillside villages, covertly making their way north and east, into the rolling countryside well outside Herod Antipas' jurisdiction. Although an overtly political program is eschewed by Jesus in the narrative of his temptations (Matthew 4.1–11; Luke 4.1–13), it is telling that he had to resist the impulse to turn himself into the king some of his followers wanted him to be (see John 6.15).

Written as they are to support the Christian practice of Eucharist in the Hellenistic world, the Gospels imbue this feeding with deeply symbolic significance. From only five loaves of bread and two fish that Jesus blessed and broke, the delegates fed the crowd, and collected remnants in twelve baskets. Twelve, the number of the clans of ancient Israel, marks the event as the promise of feeding all Israel. Within the setting of Jesus, however, the crucial decision was to attempt no insurrection in the wilderness against Antipas, but in a prophetic manner to resolve his fate in Jerusalem.

Deep controversy concerning the Temple in Jerusalem

Jesus' resolve was not to lead any military revolt, but to press for a program of climactic sacrifice in Jerusalem. The transfiguration represents a key moment of decision, in a story whose sacrificial overtones become plain when its Old Testament antecedents are observed (Matthew 16.28—17.13; Mark 9.1–13; Luke 9.27–36). Jesus is transformed before Peter, James and John – the three disciples who became preeminent in his movement immediately prior to and just after the resurrection – into a gleaming white figure, speaking with Moses and Elijah. Jesus' visions were not merely private; years of communal meditation made what he saw and experienced vivid to his own disciples as well.

On Mount Hermon, the probable location of this event, Jesus followed in the footsteps of Moses, who took three of his followers (Aaron, Nadab and Abihu) up Mount Sinai, where they ate and drank to celebrate their vision of the God of Israel on his sapphire throne (see Exodus 24.1–11). But unlike what happened on Moses' mountain, Jesus' disciples, covered by a shining cloud of glory, hear a voice, 'This is my son, the beloved, in whom I take pleasure: hear him', and when the cloud passed they found Jesus without Moses and Elijah, standing alone as God's son (Matthew 17.5). Divine 'son' was the same designation Jesus had heard during his immersion with John the Baptist (Matthew 3.13–17; Mark 1.9–11; Luke 3.21–22): now his own disciples saw and heard the truth of his vision.

In a manner symmetrical with the baptism, the voice that came after the luminous cloud in the transfiguration insisted that the same Spirit that had animated Moses and Elijah was present in Jesus, and that he could pass on that Spirit to his followers, each of whom could also become a 'son'. In the transfiguration, Peter offers to build 'huts' or 'booths' for Jesus, Moses and Elijah (Mark 9.5–6; Matthew 17.4; Luke 9.33). In so doing, Peter in his fear is presented as not knowing what to say by the Greek-speaking writers of the Gospels, but the 'huts' in question are reminiscent of those built at Sukkoth, the feast of Tabernacles. That was the sacrificial feast that, according to Zechariah 14, was to see the transformation of Israel and the world.

Attempting this sacrifice, enacting the prophecy of Zechariah, brought Jesus into direct opposition with the high priest, Caiaphas. Jesus' actual entry into Jerusalem probably took place at Sukkoth in the year 31 C.E.; that is the feast when waving and strewing branches at the altar was a regular part of processional practice (see Mark 11.8 and *Sukkah* 3.1—4.6 in the Mishnah, and the echo of 'Hosanna' of Mark 11.9 in *Sukkah* 3.9; 4.5).

The Aramaic Targum of Zechariah predicts that God's kingdom (14.9) will be manifested over the entire earth when the offerings of Sukkoth are presented by both Israelites and non-Jews at the Temple. It further predicts that these worshippers will prepare and offer their sacrifices themselves without the intervention of middlemen. The last words of the book promise, 'and there shall never again be a *trader* in the *sanctuary* of the Lord of hosts at that *time*' (Targum Zechariah 14.21, innovative wording italicized). The thrust of the Targumic prophecy brought on the dramatic confrontation that Jesus would shortly provoke in the Temple.

Enthusiastic supporters swarmed around Jesus, including his brother James. James adhered to his brother's movement once Jesus' program was defined in terms of sacrifice, rather than exorcism or military revolt. Jesus' focus on sacrifice in the Temple rather than revolt – which had perplexed the militant expectation of the '5,000' – was exactly what brought James to his side. Two things about James stand out from the principal sources from which we learn about him (Acts, Josephus and the historian Hegesippus from the second century): he never participated in armed revolt and never wavered in his loyalty to the Temple. He remained devoted to the practice of sacrifice and became famous for his piety in Jerusalem, where he was ultimately killed in 62 C.E. by a high priest who was jealous of the reverence in which he was held (Josephus, *Antiquities* 20.197–203).

Although the stratagem of Jesus, in converting a potential revolution into apocalyptic sacrifice, was brilliant at several levels, it ultimately misfired. Conflict with Caiaphas was perhaps inevitable, given Jesus' commitment to implementing the program of Zechariah. But in addition Caiaphas had newly been emboldened to change arrangements in the Temple. According to the Talmud, forty years before the destruction of the Temple (that is, during Jesus' last visit to Jerusalem), Caiaphas had expelled the Sanhedrin from their special room and place of honor called the Chamber of Hewn Stone, within the Court of the Israelites in the Temple. The Sanhedrin, consisting of priestly aristocrats, Pharisees and notables of Jerusalem, were the council of some 70 of the most important Jews in the city, who advised Caiaphas and Pilate on cultic and civic matters. They were 'exiled', as their own recollection of this expulsion put it, to Chanuth (according to the Babylonian Talmud in *Shabbat* 15a; *Sanhedrin* 41a; *Avodah Zarah* 8b), the market most likely on the Mount of Olives. That expulsion permitted Caiaphas to set up vendors in the porticos of the Temple.

Jesus' Zecharian storming of the Temple (John 2.13–16; Mark 11.15–16; Matthew 21.12; Luke 19.45) challenged Caiaphas directly, by forcing out of the Temple the trade that Caiaphas had authorized there. After his occupation of the Temple, when it became clear that he could not prevail against the high priest, Jesus denied the efficacy of sacrifice in the Temple. He called the wine and the bread of his own fellowship meal the 'blood' and 'flesh' of true sacrifice (Luke 22.15–20; Mark 14.22–25; Matthew 26.26–29). In their original setting, these words meant that Jesus set up his meals with his disciples – which were regular occasions to celebrate God's kingdom both before and after his last pilgrimage to Jerusalem – as a replacement for offerings in the Temple. Even some of his own disciples, Judas among them, were appalled by that implicit blasphemy, which played into Caiaphas' hands (John 6.60–71; 13.21–30; Matthew 26.21–25; Luke 22.21–23).

Fatefully, unknown to Jesus, the high priest's influence over the Roman prefect of the Judaea province, Pontius Pilate, was about to increase exponentially. On 18 October 31 (the same year that Jesus entered Jerusalem), the commander of the Roman imperial guard, Sejanus, had been executed in Rome. This weakened Pilate's position, because Sejanus had approved the harsh attitude of Pilate's earlier policies towards local authorities in Judaea. Pilate became more susceptible to conciliation with Caiaphas. Between then and the subsequent Passover, probably in the year 32 after a longer period than the Gospels indicate, Caiaphas managed to gain Pilate's consent to the crucifixion, with the approval of a much-relieved Antipas (Luke 23.6–12).

Attempts have been made to compute the date of the crucifixion according to when Passover fell on a Friday; that yields the familiar alternatives of 30 and 33 c.e.. But the authorities in Mark 14.2 decide to *avoid* putting Jesus to death during the feast of Passover, when the crowds would have been a threat to their plans. It appears that the calendrical association of Jesus' death and Passover is a product of the liturgical practice of Christianity, which prepared candidates for baptism during the Paschal season. Liturgy is also responsible for the presentation of the events concerning Jesus' death in a single Passion Week (between Palm Sunday and Easter).

The successful execution of Jesus, of course, did not end his influence. The conviction that God had raised him from the dead, however, went beyond the assurance that Jesus had been vindicated personally. Rather, faith in the resurrection developed the force that it did because, during his life and particularly in the midst of his last controversy in the Temple, Jesus had insisted that God was in the process of transforming society and nature to the benefit of all people, which meant that his vindication changed the nature of worship forever, and changed what would become of the world.

Bibliographical background

Study of Jesus has been well served in recent years by the multi-volume project of John P. Meier, *A Marginal Jew: Rethinking the Historical Jesus*, Anchor Bible Reference Library (New York: Doubleday, 1991 (series continued in New Haven by Yale University Press)). The perspective of this chapter reflects that work, and others that place Jesus within his environment in Judaism. That contextualization has been challenged by some scholars, who have attempted to mount the argument that Jesus was a Hellenistic thinker. The foremost representative of this school of thought in recent years has been John Dominic Crossan in, *The Historical Jesus: The Life of a Mediterranean Jewish Peasant* (San Francisco: HarperSanFrancisco, 1991). Crossan has since acknowledged that archaeological investigation has gone against his theory in a book he wrote with Jonathan L. Reed, *Excavating Jesus: Beneath the Stones, Behind the Texts* (San Francisco: HarperSanFrancisco, 2001).

Reed has been more trenchant in this regard in *Archaeology and the Galilean Jesus: A Re-examination of the Evidence* (Harrisburg, Pennsylvania: Trinity Press International, 2000). For a still more vigorous statement of how archaeology has undermined the fashion of the past few decades of scholarship, see Mark A. Chancey, *The Myth of a Gentile Galilee* (Cambridge: Cambridge University Press, 2002).

Another way of denying Jesus' Jewish environment has been the argument that scholars have only emphasized Jesus' Jewish identity in the wake of the Holocaust; see Paul Barnett, *Finding the Historical Christ* (Grand Rapids, Michigan: Eerdmans, 2009). In fact, the perspective arose with the historical critical method, an inheritance of the Reformation; see Bruce Chilton and C. A. Evans (eds), *Studying the Historical Jesus: Evaluations of the State of Current Research*, New Testament Tools and Studies 19 (Leiden: Brill, 1994 and 1998 [in paperback]).

Themes developed in this chapter rely on recent work on the *Merkavah* – see Timo Eskola, *Messiah and the Throne: Jewish Merkabah Mysticism and Early Exaltation Discourse*, Wissenschaftliche Untersuchungen zum Neuen Testament 2.142 (Tübingen: Mohr Siebeck, 2001); the Targums – see Bruce Chilton, *A Galilean Rabbi and His Bible: Jesus' Use of the Interpreted Scripture of His Time* (Wilmington, Delaware: Glazier, 1984, 216; also published with the subtitle, *Jesus' Own Interpretation of Isaiah* in London: SPCK, 1984); and the archaeological evidence regarding synagogues and *miqvaoth* – see Dan Urman and Paul V. M. Flesher (eds), *Ancient Synagogues: Historical Analysis and Archaeological Discovery*, Studia post-Biblica 4 (Leiden: Brill, 1998). Work of that kind has been applied to the question of Jesus' development in Bruce Chilton, *Rabbi Jesus: An Intimate Biography* (New York: Doubleday, 2000). Paula Fredriksen investigates the relative responsibility of Roman and Jewish authorities for Jesus' death, with particular emphasis on the Romans' intent to deter the followers of Jesus, in *Jesus of Nazareth, King of the Jews: A Jewish Life and the Emergence of Christianity* (New York: Knopf, 1999). The claim of the Gospels that Jesus was Messiah, the anointed one of God, is also found in Paul. While many writers still redefine 'Messiah' to bring it into line with their religious convictions about Jesus, the concept nonetheless coheres with Jesus' crucifixion and the inscription over the cross, 'The King of the Jews'. This discussion speaks to the question of messianic self-consciousness, which is also embedded in Jesus' relationship to the book of Zechariah; see Deirdre J. Good, *Jesus the Meek King* (Harrisburg, Pennsylvania: Trinity Press International, 1999).

Exercises

1. Birth stories

Accounts of Jesus' birth exist in the Gospels of Matthew and Luke. They share common features but differ in details. Scholars think that these narratives were added after the bulk of Gospel material had been composed. Thus it is possible to see motifs and themes in them reflected elsewhere in the Gospel and, conversely, that they encapsulate the Gospel in which they occur. Setting out the different elements of the birth stories of Matthew and Luke side by side helps to highlight the differences in their accounts (see Table 1 overleaf).

Questions

1 Are there core elements to the story of Jesus' birth in Matthew and Luke?

2 Are these core elements known to the Gospels of John or Mark?

3 What are the particular features of Matthew 1—2 and how might they be explained?

4 What are the key features of Luke's account and how might they be explained?

2. Parables

Jesus often taught his followers using parables, deceptively simple stories based in the realities of everyday life (for more on this see the box on p. 38). One parable that has been interpreted very differently by scholars is the Vineyard Workers (Matthew 20.1–16).

Questions

1 If the vineyard owner is identified with God, how might the parable be interpreted? What is the principle of justice operative in the parable? Does it resonate with ideas of justice elsewhere in Matthew's Gospel (see for example Matthew 5.20)?

2 How might the parable be interpreted from a social-scientific perspective in which the vineyard owner is a member of an oppressive elite being judged for his unfair treatment of workers? Who are the tenants and what might the message of the parable be?

3. The Lord's Prayer

The prayer that Jesus taught his disciples has become known as 'The Lord's Prayer' and is probably the best-known prayer of the Christian tradition. Read the text box 'Pray then like this...' on p. 38 and then compare these three versions of the prayer (see Table 2).

Table 1: Comparison of accounts in Matthew and Luke

Matthew 1—2 (48 verses)	Luke 1—2 (132 verses)
1.18–24 An angel tells Joseph of Jesus' birth in a dream	1.5–38 Gabriel tells Zechariah of John the Baptist's birth; then Mary of Jesus' birth
	1.39–80 Mary visits Elizabeth; John the Baptist is born and circumcised
	2.1–5 Joseph and Mary journey to Bethlehem for the census
1.25—2.1a Mary's son is born in Bethlehem of Judaea and named Jesus	2.6–7 Mary gives birth to a son in Bethlehem of Judaea
	2.8–20 Angels appear to shepherds who visit the child in a manger
	2.21 The infant is circumcised and named Jesus
1.1b–12 Magi come from the East visiting Herod then Jesus	
2.13–21 Joseph takes 'the child and his mother' to Egypt where they remain until the death of Herod	
2.22–23 They return to Israel and settle in Nazareth to fulfil prophecies	2.39–40 The trio returns to Nazareth
	2.41–52 A teenage Jesus and extended family visit the Jerusalem Temple

Table 2: The Lord's Prayer

Matthew 6.9–15	*Luke 11.1–4*	*Didache 8.2*
Our Father, the one in the heavens	Father,	Our Father, the one in the heaven
Hallowed be your name	Hallowed be your name	Hallowed be your name
Your kingdom come. Your will be done on earth as it is in heaven.	Your kingdom come.	Your kingdom come. Your will be done on earth as it is in heaven.
Give us this day our daily bread;	Give us each day our daily bread;	Give us this day our bread for the morrow;
And forgive us our debts, as we also have forgiven our debtors;	And forgive us our sins, for we ourselves forgive everyone who is indebted to us;	And forgive us our sin as we forgive those who sin against us;
And lead us not into temptation but deliver us from evil.	And lead us not into temptation.	And lead us not into temptation but deliver us from evil. For the power and glory are yours forever.

Questions

1 What are the differences between these three versions of the Lord's Prayer?

2 Why is the Lord's Prayer absent from Mark's and John's Gospels?

3 Summarize the content of the prayer. Are there specifically Christian elements (compare e.g. Exodus 3.14; Psalm 145; Ezekiel 36.20–23)? Could you imagine someone Jewish praying this prayer today?

4. The last words of Jesus

Jesus' last words before he died on the cross were considered significant by each of the Gospel writers. However, they each record his words differently:

- Mark 15.34: At three o'clock Jesus cried out with a loud voice, 'Eloi, Eloi, lema sabachthani?' which means, 'My God, my God, why have you forsaken me?'

51

- Matthew 27.46: And about three o'clock Jesus cried with a loud voice, 'Eli, Eli, lema sabachthani?' that is, 'My God, my God, why have you forsaken me?'
- Luke 23.46: Then Jesus, crying with a loud voice, said, 'Father, into your hands I commend my spirit.' Having said this, he breathed his last.
- John 19.28–30: After this, when Jesus knew that all was now finished, he said (in order to fulfil the Scripture), 'I am thirsty.' A jar full of sour wine was standing there. So they put a sponge full of the wine on a branch of hyssop and held it to his mouth. When Jesus had received the wine, he said, 'It is finished.' Then he bowed his head and gave up his spirit.

Questions

1 Does it make a difference to the reader's understanding of Mark and Matthew if Jesus' words seem to be quoting Psalm 22?

2 Why do Gospels written in Greek preserve Aramaic words of Jesus? Where else does this happen and what is its significance? (Begin by looking at the following passages: Mark 5.41; 14.36.)

3 How do you account for the variations among Jesus' last words as reported in the Gospels?

Further reading

M. A. Beavis (ed.), *The Lost Coin: Parables of Women, Work and Wisdom* (London/New York: Sheffield Academic Press, 2002)

Mark A. Chauncy, *Greco-Roman Culture and the Galilee of Jesus*, Society of New Testament Studies Monograph Series 134 (Cambridge: Cambridge University Press, 2005)

Bruce Chilton, *Jesus' Prayer and Jesus' Eucharist: His Personal Practice of Spirituality* (Valley Forge, Pennsylvania: Trinity Press International, 1997)

Elizabeth M. Dowling and W. George Scarlett (eds), *Encyclopedia of Religious and Spiritual Development* (Thousand Oaks, California: Sage, 2006), 'Lord's Prayer', 267–9

Richard A. Horsley, *Archaeology, History and Society in Galilee: The Social Context of Jesus and the Rabbis* (Valley Forge, Pennsylvania: Trinity Press International, 1996)

Klyne R. Snodgrass, *Stories with Intent: A Comprehensive Guide to the Parables of Jesus* (Grand Rapids, Michigan: Eerdmans, 2008)

Joan Taylor, *The Immerser: John the Baptist within Second Temple Judaism, Studying the Historical Jesus* (Grand Rapids: Eerdmans, 1997)

Geza Vermes, *The Complete Dead Sea Scrolls in English* (New York and London: Penguin, 2004)

Figure 3. Ephesus Theater: The Emperor Augustus made Ephesus the capital of the Roman province of Asia, in which it became the preeminent city in commercial, cultural, and philosophical terms despite a destructive earthquake in 23 C.E. Acts 19 describes Paul's effect on the city, reflecting the realities of a sizeable Jewish population (although a synagogue has yet to be located), a thriving market in idols connected with a monumental temple to Artemis, and serious differences among Christian preachers. *Photo by Norman Herr, courtesy of Wikimedia Commons (public domain inage).*

2

Paul and his letters

Paul is one of history's transformative figures. He came not from the territory of ancient Israel but from the Diaspora, a term in Greek that means 'dispersion' and refers to the fact that, by the first century, many more Jews lived outside Israel than within that territory. Many of these families, like Paul's, had lived within their new cultures for generations, and contributed to the diverse cultural mix of what is called the Hellenistic world. In the wake of the conquests of Alexander the Great, Greek became the common language of the Mediterranean Basin and the Near East, and the culture of the Greeks (the *Hellenes*) cross-pollinated with a wide variety of influences throughout that area.

Paul wove his devotion to Israel together with the Stoic philosophy of the Hellenistic world, a school of thought that searched for a single, rational principle underneath the world of nature as well as human society. On that basis, Paul framed a new perspective on the meaning of Jesus as the exemplar and the hope of all humanity. Before the word Christianity gained currency (a term that Paul himself never used in his letters), Paul made following Jesus into a radically new and powerful religious movement.

Paul's influence over the Church grew with time. The Protestant Reformation based its comprehensive program of reform on his thought. For all the vehemence of its stand against Protestantism, Roman Catholic Christianity since the Second Vatican Council has increasingly emphasized Paul's teaching that God's favor cannot be earned by obedience to convention, and Orthodox Christianity has always venerated 'the Apostle'.

Paul's critics – ancient and modern – have pilloried Paul, making him responsible for whatever is wrong with Christianity. They have portrayed Paul as anti-feminist, homophobic and doctrinaire – while fundamentalist Christians, who attempt to embrace biblical teaching as literal and inerrant truth, often embrace such attitudes as part of their Pauline inheritance. Paul's own letters give some support to this picture. He wrote that women in Corinth should shut up in church (1 Corinthians 14.33–35); he despised homosexual prostitution (1 Corinthians 6.9–10, where the language in Greek implies commercial sex); at times he employed crude language to insist he alone was right (Galatians 5.12).

The New Testament gives us Paul's life and thought in fragments. His letters are the earliest documents in the New Testament, when they are genuine. But some that have traditionally been attributed to Paul were not written by him (such as Hebrews and Titus), and one of the most important of the authentic letters (2 Corinthians) is pasted together from separate pieces of correspondence. Even when we have whole and genuine letters, we are in the position of an eavesdropper who can hear only one side of a conversation, since we don't have letters written back to Paul. We need to parse his words to assess the issues he is addressing and from what perspective, and we have to gather the settings and milieux that he addressed from what he says about them.

In this task the Acts of the Apostles remains a valuable resource, along with archaeology and ancient histories. A broad consensus of scholars puts the writing of Acts around 90 c.e. if not later, about thirty years after Paul had stopped writing. But the writer of Acts clearly incorporated earlier material in his narrative. Many details in Acts correspond to historical and archaeological evidence. Acts is not more reliable than Paul's letters, but its presentation merits assessment. Sometimes there is good reason to infer that Paul keeps a self-interested silence that Acts breaks, while sometimes Acts' mythic convictions – of peace and unanimity in the early Church, for example – are simply implausible.

Perpetually restless, reckless with his own life and sometimes with the lives of others, Paul travelled around the Mediterranean – Asia Minor, Judaea, Syria, Greece and Italy – challenging synagogues, forums and fledgling churches, making friends and breaking friendships. To trace his complex itinerary requires logical inference. Historians *infer* from evidence, and do not really 'prove' anything in a scientific or mathematical sense. That is a well-established principle in the study of history.

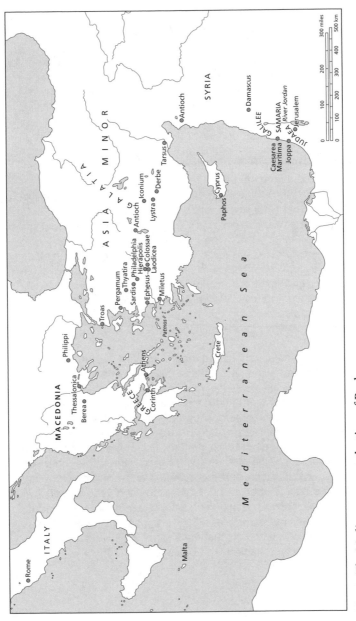

Map 2 The Mediterranean at the time of Paul

Box 2.1. Interpreting New Testament texts

When we interpret New Testament texts, we have a theory of interpretation. While an author is no longer available to be questioned, the world of the author is. So meaning may be derived from an investigation of what the author of a biblical text intends to convey, alongside what the text articulates, and how the reader perceives the text. To emphasize author, reader or text at the expense of one of the other three is to impoverish the process of interpretation. (For more on this see the Introduction, pp. 5–6).

At the same time, different interpreters can emphasize one element of the approach, giving it particular weight. Some scholars use scholarship only to yield information about the historical Jesus or genuine Paul in the letters as opposed to the Paul of Acts. Texts are deployed for ancient facts and their ancient contexts. Older scholarship proposed to uncover an author's intention through sources the author used (source criticism), textual forms in which authorial expression took place (form criticism) and motifs particular to a piece of writing indicating an author's editorial interests and features (redaction criticism).

Other scholars stress the reader as creator and determiner of textual meaning. Still others fall somewhere in between, arguing that interpretation must take account of a recovery of historical context of both text and author on the one hand, while at the same time acknowledging contemporary insights from literary criticism about the role of the reader.

Objectivity cannot be claimed for any of these emphases at the expense of the others. And since any interpreter operates in a particular time and place, and since any interpreta-tion takes author, text and reader into account in various ways, we must recognize that this search for meaning is open-ended, contingent and incomplete. The process of interpretation is never over. This means that the search for meaning produces results more probable than absolute.

Tarsus and Jerusalem

The Jews of Tarsus – a prosperous city in the country today called Turkey – could freely pursue trades, tent-making among them. This skilled craft required expertise and tools, and investment in people and material, to work the leather and felt from which tents were made. The investment offered excellent prospects: any army or caravan of traders had need of professionals to get their camps set up and keep them in good repair.

Paul's family in Tarsus in all likelihood brought him up in this trade (Acts 18.1–3). As prominent citizens of Tarsus – and Roman citizens (Acts 21.39; 22.25–28) – they shared in the huge tax advantage that Rome had given the city, and profitable contacts came their way. As citizens, they were expected to extend their patronage to the city, but they had means enough to do that without difficulty. Citizenship was well worth the expense in terms of the commercial advantages it gave: access to business with the Roman army and magistracy.

Wealthy men such as Paul's father could afford real mansions with courtyards, space for the extended family, and servants' quarters. We can't estimate the size of Paul's family exactly, but the book of Acts does mention a sister whose son was in Jerusalem when Paul was arrested there towards the end of his life (Acts 23.16). Wealth would have meant Paul's parents could beat the odds of infant mortality better than most; he probably had several brothers and sisters. Because Paul freely travelled to Jerusalem once he had grown, it seems unlikely he was the only son, or even the eldest son. Paul's father would have assured the stability of the family and its business (including his commercial successor) before he allowed number two or three son to dance to the beat of distant drummers.

Paul needed this support to pursue his unusual vocation to train as a Pharisee in Jerusalem, which he detailed in one of his later letters, Philippians. In addition to referring to being a Pharisee, he said (Philippians 3.4–5) that he had been circumcised on the eighth day and was a true Israelite by parentage, birth and practice, not merely an admirer of Judaism. He was descended from the clan of Benjamin, at least, his family maintained, and spoke Aramaic as well as Greek. By means of his family and their synagogue, he was acculturated as a Jew in a thoroughly Hellenistic city.

When Paul attached himself to the Pharisees (Philippians 3.5), they became an intellectual influence on him at the earliest stage of his adult life. Pharisaism was originally a movement in Jerusalem; its aim was to influence the conduct of worship and sacrifice in the Temple. Outright control of the Temple's operation eluded the Pharisees, but they did manage to infiltrate the city council in Jerusalem (the Sanhedrin). Outside Jerusalem, initially in cities and towns of Judaea and Galilee, some Pharisees also pursued their agenda by urging Jews to maintain the kind of purity in daily life that would make them fit to participate in worship in the Temple. Although the Temple was far away, Pharisees convinced their followers, even in the Diaspora, that the spiritual benefit of belonging to Israel would be theirs, if they would observe the basic requirements that God set out in the Torah: 'You shall be holy, because I am holy' (Leviticus 19.2). The Pharisees persuaded local populations to immerse themselves for purification in the kinds of bathing pools they mandated (called *miqvaoth*), to observe regulations of tithing, and to exert particular care in the storage and preparation of foods. In all of this, the purity of the Pharisaic household was analogous to the ideals the Pharisees desired to see realized in the Temple.

Paul's devotion to the Temple as the center of purity and sacrifice brought him to persecute followers of Jesus. The members of the Sanhedrin who had agreed in 32 c.e. that Jesus should be denounced to Pilate did so because Jesus had stormed into the Temple with his followers, disrupting its operation. Caiaphas had personal grounds for animosity, but any Israelite might well have been offended by Jesus' raid. After Jesus' activity in the Temple made him a hunted man, he started to call the wine he shared with his disciples during meals his 'blood', and the bread his 'flesh', as if those meals supplanted offerings in the Temple in God's sight. In Jerusalem, as in Galilee, Jesus' meals with his followers were repeated, and their meaning was inextricable from his purpose overall. His continued activity in offering his disciples a surrogate for sacrifice seemed to upholders of the status quo an insult to the Temple. By that stage, enough people on the council agreed with Caiaphas, despite the reluctance of people such as Joseph of Arimathea, so that Jesus could be identified to Pilate as a threat to the public order and Rome's hegemony.

To a young Pharisee such as Paul, assaults on arrangements authorized by the high priest threatened covenantal worship in the sanctuary, and talk of meals replacing Temple sacrifice was blasphemous. The focus of God's presence was the Temple, on the mercy seat over the ark, where men of Paul's discipline regularly devoted their prayers and their thoughts, as well as their sacrifices. Stephen, a Greek-speaking Jew and a prominent follower of Jesus in Jerusalem, announced that Jesus' authority was greater than the Temple's. Paul, never one to take things lightly, was revolted, and he joined in the stoning of Stephen (Acts 7.54–60).

Paul acknowledges his previous anti-Christian activity with regret (Galatians 1.13; 1 Corinthians 15.9; Philippians 3.6). But at the time what he did was more *for* the Temple than *against* Jesus; from the temple the recognition of the one, true God radiated to the whole Diaspora. Acts even portrays Paul as taking letters to Damascus on behalf of the high priest, ordering the arrest of Christians there (Acts 9.1–2). That attributes more direct power to Caiaphas outside of Jerusalem than he actually possessed, but it is plausible that the high priest communicated with synagogues in Damascus, asking members to denounce followers of Jesus there to the Romans. For this purpose, he needed educated zealots, as they were called at the time (Galatians 1.14), militant ideologues who could deliver, read, explain and defend the letters he sent out, both in Aramaic and in Greek. Paul was an ideal candidate, with the added cachet of his nascent standing with the Pharisaic movement and the cultural advantage, from his upbringing in Tarsus, of being bilingual.

The call

Twenty years after his experience near Damascus, Paul explained the meaning of his conversion in his own words (Galatians 1.15–16): 'When it pleased the one who separated me from my mother's belly and called me through his grace to uncover his Son in me so that I should announce his triumph among the Gentiles, at first I did not confer with flesh and blood.' This revelation was prophetic. Like a prophet, Paul felt he had been predestined to this moment from his 'mother's belly' (Jeremiah 1.5; Isaiah 49.1–6). The unveiling of God's Son within him took priority over any human contact or circumstance.

Paul puts the deep content of this experience economically: God determined 'to uncover his Son in' him. The term 'uncover' (*apokalupsai*) in Greek is typically rendered 'reveal' in English versions of the Bible. By the same token, the noun *apokalupsis*, our 'apocalypse', becomes 'revelation'. These translations make readers think in terms of external stimuli coming to the seer like ordinary sense perceptions. The basic meaning of this language, however, is that a heavenly mystery has its cover (its -*kalupsis*) taken off (*apo*-): the veil of circumstance is momentarily stripped from spiritual reality. Here the cover is removed from God's Son, who is 'in' (Greek: *en*) Paul, within his consciousness in an experience uniquely his.

Paul's experience was not of an objective event that other people shared fully. He alone was converted that day. His brief reference in Galatians relates to a personal moment of disclosure, an unveiling of the divine. He conceived of his mystical breakthrough in ways rooted in his mixed background, pagan and Jewish.

Many Stoics in Tarsus were taken up with the possibility of people moving beyond knowledge of the divine, and becoming divine themselves. Cicero – a famous Stoic philosopher who briefly governed the region of Tarsus a half-century before Paul was born – voiced this hope for exaltation to the divine world. The popular source of early Judaism called the book of *Enoch* reflected a similar longing in visionary terms, and shows how the God of Israel could fulfil Stoic aspirations. Paul the Stoic felt, like the Stoic philosopher Athenodorus of Tarsus, that humanity could be linked into a single body by a divine principle (1 Corinthians 12.12–27), and that prayer and behaviour should be open to the light of day (1 Thessalonians 5.4–9). In a well-worn Stoic image, he compared himself to a runner competing for a prize (1 Corinthians 9.24–27), a spectacle that his youth in Tarsus offered him. Similarly, it was both as a Stoic and as a Jew that Paul spoke of the uncovering of God's Son, the principle of divinity, within him. Yet at the same time, Paul all his life reflected popular customs from his upbringing that were local to the point of being parochial. For example, Paul believed in maturity, as he had been taught in Tarsus, that it was shameful for a woman not to be covered in public, and intemperately said she ought to have all her hair shorn off her head if she disagreed (1 Corinthians 11.5–6).

Diverse influences are evident in Paul's conceptions. Two thousand years of Christianity makes us think instantly of Jesus when we hear of the 'Son of God'. But the phrase had a life of its own before it was applied to Jesus, referring to angels (Genesis 6.2), the whole people called Israel (Hosea 11.1), and the king in David's line (Psalm 2.7), while Stoics referred to the Roman emperor as God's 'Son', in the sense that he represented the rational principle in the whole of the Roman empire.

When Paul felt the divine 'Son' uncovered within himself, he encountered a revelation that replaced his Pharisaic focus on the presence of God in the Temple. As angels had once guided Cicero and Enoch, a supernatural guide, the divine Son, brought Paul to the heaven within himself. That is why the answer to his question, 'Who are you, Lord?' came as the most terrifying thing Paul ever heard. 'I am Jesus, whom you persecute!' (Acts 26.15). No response could have agonized him more. Profound loyalty to the Temple, not malice, had led Paul to serve Caiaphas, to resist the malcontents from Galilee and the Diaspora who claimed that their dead rabbi's authority trumped the high priest's. Yet now this angelic Son of God identified himself as Jesus, raised from the dead.

Disciples of Jesus cared for Paul, and he recovered the sight his vision had cost him for more than three days (Acts 9.9, 18). He unwisely began right away to announce in synagogues that Jesus was the divine Son, prompting hostile scepticism. People knew about the stoning of Stephen, and knew this budding Pharisee from the Diaspora had travelled to Damascus to denounce those baptized in Jesus' name. That's what prompted their taunt (Acts 9.21): 'Isn't he the one who laid waste in Jerusalem to those calling upon this name, and came here for this purpose?' Why should they accept the word of an interloper who remade himself so readily from a Jerusalem Pharisee one day, into a follower of 'the way', as followers of Jesus called their movement, another day? From this juncture Paul made *his* way, always a minority way in his lifetime, but gradually the main line of Christianity.

The apostle

The depth of Paul's change as he made his way to Damascus merits the name of conversion, because it involved a literal turn around (*conversio* in Latin) of his previous attitude towards Jesus and his movement. Paul believed that the God of Israel, by raising one human being from the dead, his Son Jesus, made all people of faith – even non-Jews – into the people of God. Jesus, the emblem of divine presence within humanity, had become the most inclusive and profound connection between God and human beings in Paul's mind. Even the Torah God had given Moses, binding on Jews but not on Gentiles, was only of incidental importance as compared to the revelation of the Son of God.

Paul came to this insight, now a standard aspect of Christian faith, before anyone else. His teaching brought controversy that was only exacerbated by the knowledge that Paul once persecuted the faith that he now preached. For years, between his departure from Jerusalem (Acts 9.26–30) and when he was called to a new apostolic field (Acts 11.25–26), he returned to relative obscurity in Tarsus. But then events conspired to make his unique perspective useful.

In Antioch on the Orontes river in Syria, large numbers of non-Jews started to be baptized into Jesus' movement. Peter had endorsed sporadic conversions by pagan God-fearers, that is non-Jews who acknowledged the God of Israel without keeping all the laws of purity, as exceptions to the rule of Jewish identity (Acts 10.1–48). But who would live in non-Jewish communities on a regular basis to bring the message of Jesus to pagans? In order to deal with them Paul was brought to Antioch by the apostle Barnabas, also a Jew from the Diaspora (Acts 11.19–25).

In Antioch, the inevitable question arose: could Gentiles truly convert to the movement of Jesus without keeping the Law of Moses? Paul insisted that they could, but some Christian teachers – from the Pharisees, the same party that had produced Paul himself (Acts 15.5) – countered that the Law was explicit (see Genesis 17.9–14): only those who kept the covenant of circumcision, and all the rules of purity and morality that implied, belonged to the people of God. A meeting among the chief leaders of Jesus' followers at the time, headed by James, Jesus' brother, and including Peter and Barnabas and Paul, came to a compromise. Gentiles, they decided, could indeed receive baptism while remaining Gentiles (Acts 15.1–18; Galatians 2.1–5), but the attempt to bring Gentiles into the Church would not be pressed on traditionally Jewish lands. Instead, geography would separate Gentile believers from Jewish believers, so that Paul's missionary effort among pagans was to press to the west (Galatians 2.6–10), where prophecy said (Isaiah 66.18–23) that non-Jews would come to faith in Israel's God.

Paul's letters

1 Thessalonians

1 Thessalonians is chronologically the first of Paul's letters, which he wrote with Silas and Timothy. Paul takes the lead in addressing the community at Thessalonica because it principally comprised Gentile Christians. In the way of first efforts, there is a tentative quality here compared to Paul's later letters. The three teachers say that their message comes from God's own Spirit (1.5) and focuses on Jesus as divine Son, who alone can deliver humanity from the rapidly approaching end of the ages (1.10).

This eschatological tenor is typical of primitive Christianity, and characterizes Paul's letters. Time is truly short, because the day of the Lord comes as a thief in the night (5.2), at a time that cannot be reckoned. In view of this up-coming judgment, the Thessalonian Gentiles had put their idols aside (1.9), and that also meant (as Paul is never slow to point out) that sexual sanctification had to follow. Lust was a reflex of idolatry: now was the time for 'every one of you to keep one's own vessel in sanctification and honor, and not in the passion of lust just like the Gentiles who do not know God' (4.4–5). The three teachers agreed that turning from idolatry and perversion to serve the living God was the only means of human salvation in the short time before the Day of Judgment. Baptized Gentiles were not obliged to keep the Torah in the way that Israelites were, but basic loyalty to God as the one divine power remained fundamental.

1 Thessalonians also fiercely states that the Pharisaic teachers from Judaea who had tried to prevent contact with Gentiles formed an obstacle to the gospel (2.14): 'For you, brothers, became imitators of

the churches of God that are in Judaea in Jesus Christ, because you also suffered the same things from your kinspeople as they did from the Jews.' This refers back to the deep contention in Jerusalem. Paul, Silas and Timothy are using the word 'Jews' (*Ioudaioi* in Greek) to mean followers of 'the way' back in Judaea who wished to 'forbid us to speak to the Gentiles' (2.16). But the same term could also be used during the first century (and later, of course) to refer to practitioners of Judaism anywhere, and that is the sense of the term 'Jew' in usage. So the three companions, writing to Thessalonica and dealing with local issues and recent history, spoke in a way that later encouraged anti-Semitism.

Galatians

By the time Paul wrote entirely on his own, in his letter to the Galatians, he had changed. But circumstances in Jerusalem had also changed, and they were changing even more drastically in Antioch. Between Paul's visit to Jerusalem in 46 C.E. and his pilgrimage in 52 C.E., James' position had grown stronger, and he had become dubious of Paul's theology. Paul's teaching that all believers, whether Jewish or not, belonged to Israel was a radical departure, and Paul had nearly been killed by stoning in Lystra (Acts 14.1–20).

James simply disagreed with Paul: Gentiles baptized in Jesus' name without circumcision were not Israelites, in his view, but a people called by God to support and sustain Israel. To insist on this, James decided to send an encyclical to believing Gentiles commanding them 'to abstain from the pollutions of the idols, and from fornication, and from what is strangled, and from blood' (Acts 15.20). The Torah's specific requirements for Jews in particular (for example, circumcision and dietary regulations) could not be imposed on Gentiles, but accepting the God of Israel implied acknowledging that parts of the Torah spoke to humanity as a whole.

The rules set out by James tended naturally to separate believing Gentiles from pagans. They had to refrain from feasts in honor of the gods and from foods sacrificed to idols in the course of being butchered and sold, although the devotion of animals in the market to one god or another was common practice in the Hellenistic world. They had to observe stricter limits than usual on the type of sexual activity they might engage in, and with whom: marriage with close relatives was fashionable in the Hellenistic world, but forbidden in the book of Leviticus (18.6–18). They had to avoid the flesh of animals that had been strangled instead of bled, because that method of slaughter left blood in the meat, and they were not to consume blood itself. These strictures are consistent with James' position at the time he decided Gentile believers did not have to be circumcised: God had co-opted a people from the Gentiles (Acts 15.14), and now he said they had to be similar to Israel and supportive of Israel. His decree fatefully left open the question, whether believing Gentiles – if they kept James' rules of purity – would be able to eat with believing Jews at common meals. Events would prove that James himself did not permit that practice, but those same events – as interpreted by Paul – directly challenged James' authority.

Paul never accepted all the requirements James imposed on believing Gentiles. Yet even Peter, in Antioch to promote the baptism of Gentiles who accepted James' strictures, accepted the decree of James – as did Barnabas, the most prestigious Christian resident of the city. Paul, newly returned to Antioch, stood alone.

Acts does not report the confrontation at all. It was too embarrassing for that book's portrait of primitive Christian unity. Paul, on the other hand, not only reported the dispute, but proudly related his part in it (Galatians 2.11–13):

> But when Cephas [the Aramaic for Peter, meaning 'rock'] came to Antioch, I stood up against him to his face, because he was condemned. Because before some came from James, he used to eat with the Gentiles. But when they came, he backed away and separated himself, fearing those of the circumcision. And the rest of the Jews were made hypocrites with him – so that even Barnabas was carried away with their hypocrisy.

Fired by his passion for his own opinion, Paul calls *any* appeal to ancestral Judaism 'circumcision', as if not eating blood were the same thing. When Peter and Barnabas fall in with the policy of James in regard to purity, Paul calls that a hypocritical fear of the circumcision backers (Galatians 2.11–13); when unnamed teachers actually urge circumcision on Gentiles, Paul tells them to cut their own genitals off (Galatians 5.1–12). This is in sharp contrast to the Paul who had once eagerly desired James' approval for his mission. In his language, all who disagree with him are circumcisers, whether they really want circumcision or not.

Paul's anger is a matter of principle as well as passion. He insisted that, because believers *were* Israel, *in toto*, they had to eat with one another, whatever James said. What Paul was asking for was completely consistent with his own position, but untenable on the basis of traditional Judaism, for which the separation of Jews and non-Jews was axiomatic. As he said himself, he was opposed by Peter, Barnabas, the envoys of James, and 'the rest of the Jews' (Galatians 2.13). Paul left Antioch, Barnabas and Peter remained. The decree of James carried the day, and Paul was now effectively an excommunicant from his own movement.

That experience helps explain the vehemence of Paul's letter to the Galatians of Asia Minor, which he wrote from Ephesus, his new center of operations. He was incensed because the non-Jewish believers in Galatia that he had initiated into the Spirit of Christ were now willing to accept circumcision, keep the calendar of Judaism and accept the strictures of James about what they could eat, how and with whom. His crude language reflects the virulence of his feelings. People who want to circumcise Gentiles for the sake of Christ should just 'cut off' their own genitals (Galatians 5.12); keeping the festivals and Sabbaths of Judaism is as bad as serving idols (Galatians 4.8–11); observing purity at meals is hypocrisy (Galatians 2.13). He blasted any gesture by Gentile Christians towards an acceptance of Judaism.

Paul's thought had evolved to the point that he spoke of the Torah as an obstacle to the message of Christ. The antithesis between Spirit and flesh, between gospel and custom, between divine grace and human intention, was basic to Paul's position, because of his experience on the road to Damascus. Christ appeared to him as the triumph of Spirit over every convention, even the Torah. That experience explains Paul's famous teaching of justification by faith – the pivot on which the Reformation turned. He articulates what he means by spelling out how he sees the uncovering of

God's Son within the believer as superseding the place of the Torah (2.19–21):

> For I through the Law am dead to the Law, that I might live in God. I have been crucified with Christ. I live – yet no longer I – but Christ lives in me. And the life I now live in flesh, I live by the faith of God's Son, who loved me and gave himself for me. I do not refuse the grace of God; for if righteousness were through law, the Christ died for nothing.

1 and 2 Corinthians

A natural extension of Paul's position in regard to the Torah would find resort to the law as such (whether Moses' law or any other mandate) as antithetical to Christ. Yet Paul himself did not draw that conclusion. He believed that the Torah remained an imperative for Jews, and he also believed that even non-Jewish believers were guided by the Spirit to maintain what Paul called 'the law of Christ' (Galatians 6.2). He worked out this aspect of his thought especially in his letters to the diverse Christian communities of Corinth. Divisions among those groups threatened to undermine Paul's teaching that all believers receive a single Spirit. He let his temper show when he said (1 Corinthians 1.13): 'Is Christ divided? Was Paul crucified for you, or were you baptized in Paul's name?' Paul stakes his claim to authority on the basis of the disclosure of Christ that brings the Spirit. Spirit, in his mind, was the one substance that could endure the judgment that was to come (1 Corinthians 3.10–17).

1 Corinthians is, in literary terms, Paul's greatest achievement, perhaps the finest single piece of writing in the New Testament. It reaches one of its heights, beautifully coordinated to the specific circumstances addressed, in the description of the Church as the body of Christ, animated by a single, divine Spirit (1 Corinthians 12.12–30) that guides believers better than the Torah. To his mind, therefore, it was unthinkable for a man to marry a woman who had been his father's wife (1 Corinthians 5.1). This was off the chart of permissible behaviour even 'among the Gentiles' and violated Paul's principle that everyone should 'keep one's own vessel in sanctification and honor, and not in the passion of lust just like the Gentiles who do not know God' (1 Thessalonians 4.4–5).

Box 2.2. Timeline of Paul's letters

50   Paul met with Priscilla and Aquila in Corinth (Acts 18.2; 1 Corinthians 16.19) after Claudius' expulsion of many Jews from Rome in 49 C.E.. From Corinth, Paul, Silas and Timothy wrote to the Thessalonians.

1 July, 51–1 July, 52   The tenure of Gallio in Corinth (Acts 18.12). In Paul's absence, a meeting in Jerusalem – sealed by a decree from James – stipulates requirements of purity for Gentile believers. Later in 52, the penultimate journey of Paul to Jerusalem (Acts 18.22).

53   The confrontation at Antioch, occasioned by the decree of James (Galatians 2.11–21; and Acts 15.19–24).

53–56   Paul's period in Ephesus (with a retreat to Macedonia and Troas at the end); the composition of Galatians, 1 Corinthians and 2 Corinthians.

57   Letter to the Romans, written from Miletus off the coast from Ephesus, and final arrangements for the Sacrifice of the Nations. Paul's arrest in Jerusalem and detention in Caesarea.

58   The composition of Philemon the following year.

59–62   Festus' tenure, overlapping with the end of that of the high priest, Ananias (Acts 25—26). Paul's appeal to the Philippians for help in his letter to that city, written with Timothy and later expanded by Timothy.

62   Paul's release, his final period in Rome, and the composition of poetry later incorporated by Timothy in the letter to the Colossians.

64   Paul's death in Rome under Nero.

73   The burning of the Temple by the Roman troops under Titus; the composition of Mark's Gospel in Rome; the end of the revolt against Rome in Palestine.

75   Josephus publishes his *Jewish War*.

80   The composition of Matthew's Gospel, in Damascus.

90   The composition of Luke's Gospel and Acts, in Antioch. Timothy's release of letters written by Paul with his help, together with the Epistle to the Ephesians. The Pastoral Epistles were composed later in the same decade.

93   Josephus publishes his *Antiquities of the Jews*.

95   The Epistle to the Hebrews.

Paul passes judgment on the Corinthians *in absentia* (1 Corinthians 5.3–5):

> For absent in body but present in the Spirit, I have already judged – as being present – the man who has behaved this way. In the name of our Lord Jesus, when you have gathered and my spirit is with the power of our Lord Jesus – turn over such a man to Satan for destruction of the flesh, so that the spirit might be saved in the day of the Lord.

The eloquent and authoritative appeal for unity in 1 Corinthians is superseded in 2 Corinthians, when Paul compares his apostolic colleagues to Satan, 'who disguised himself as an angel of light' (2 Corinthians 11.14). He dismissed his competitors as servants of the god of this world of passing flesh. Paul insisted that only he was right, and that the authority of any other apostles was to be exorcized from Corinth. His confidence is grounded in his eschatological authority to speak on behalf of the spiritual world that was coming to replace the world of flesh. At the same time, Paul by this stage had to contend with the reality that his opposition to idolatry in Ephesus made his position there untenable (Acts 19.23–41; 1 Corinthians 15.32) and local outrage at his rejection of idols forced him to flee.

Romans

In his letter to the Romans, Paul tied many of these themes together and approached writing a synthesis of his thought. He dictated this letter to Rome in Miletus in 57 c.e., prior to setting out for his final pilgrimage to Jerusalem. He polished this letter thoroughly; despite arrest and deep conflict with communities he had been attached to (including those in Corinth), he remained confident. The tone differs deliberately from the volatile correspondence with Corinth. In Romans, Paul is writing a letter of introduction for himself, seeking to establish a relationship such as he had enjoyed in Ephesus with a new city – the greatest city in his world.

Paul here sounds the familiar motif of Christ as a corporate, all-embracing 'body' (Romans 12.4–8), but with a new economy of words, and deploys the classic Stoic trope that earthly rulers are divine ministers 'for the good' (13.1–4). He could take this position because he knew that obedience to any political authority was as temporary as this world. His position was also tactical: by using the language and ideas of Stoicism to describe the cosmic reach of Christ's revelation, and by insisting that faith was consistent with imperial law, Paul legitimated Christianity's place in philosophical discourse and helped make the claim for its political legitimacy as well.

Romans closes with Paul's plan for his visit to Jerusalem, where he proposed to complete what he called his 'priestly service'. He intended to take contributions from Gentile believers in order to bring sacrifice in the Temple, 'so that the offering of the Gentiles might become acceptable to God, sanctified by the Holy Spirit' (Romans 15.16). Jesus would indeed become what Paul calls the sacrificial place (the *hilasterion*) where God would take pleasure in the offering of every human being (3.21–25):

> And now apart from Law God's righteousness has been manifested, attested by the Law and the Prophets – God's righteousness through Christ Jesus' faith for all who believe. There is no distinction. For all have sinned and lack the glory of God, yet are made righteous as a gift by his grace through the redemption that is in Jesus Christ, whom God appointed a place of sacrifice through faith in his blood . . .

Christ for Paul is the *hilasterion* because he provides the occasion for true worship, an opportunity for the eschatological sacrifice in Jerusalem, the same city in which Jesus shed his blood. Jews and Greeks could indeed offer sacrifice together in Christ (without 'distinction'), joined in mutual recognition that the blood he shed was not Jewish blood or Greek blood, but the human suffering that God has decided to transcend.

Paul's last visit to Jerusalem

Political and religious complications awaited Paul in Jerusalem. He had arrived there with non-Jews in his entourage (Acts 21.27–29), so it was all too easy for Jewish worshippers in the Temple, seeing Paul with a large group of supporters, to suppose that the leading apostle of the non-Jews had finally consummated his blasphemy by bringing Gentiles into the inner sanctuary that was prohibited to non-Israelites. Introducing Gentiles into the interior Temple reserved for

Israel was a sacrilege punishable by death, and a mob in the Temple rioted against Paul (Acts 21.28). The Roman army intervened, and Paul's arrest made him appeal to judgment in Rome itself.

For the first time in his life, as he awaited his appeal in Rome, Paul relied entirely on other people for his daily needs. Custody for a citizen did not involve punitive imprisonment (Acts 28.16), but payments for his housing, food, serving staff, guardians, and occasional bribes to officials quickly depleted Paul's funds. He ate up his remaining 'offering of the Gentiles' by rendering Caesar his due, and then had to turn to his friends. His sacrifice had proven a failure. This was not just the world's rejection; the Temple had spurned him.

Paul's letters after his arrest

Philemon

Paul needed deep relationships to sustain him. Timothy became his closest friend. He increasingly spoke for Paul, and composed letters with him in which he also expressed his own concerns. In 58 c.e., Paul and Timothy wrote a private letter to a wealthy slaveholder they had met back in Ephesus named Philemon. Paul's whole concern in these 25 short verses is with a slave Philemon had loaned him, named Onesimus (vv. 8–10):

> So having much confidence in Christ to order you what is proper, for love's sake I rather appeal – being Paul the senior, but now also a prisoner for Jesus Christ – I appeal to you concerning my child, whom I begat in my bonds, Onesimus . . .

The whole focus is Paul's deep attachment to Onesimus, a feeling he experiences, he says, deep in his body: his viscera (*splangkhna* in Greek).

Philippians

Timothy is named as a co-writer of the letter to the Philippians as well, written when he and Paul put into Myra on the way to Rome. Paul's affection suffuses this letter, as well as his deliberate emphasis on how to concentrate his thoughts on people in Philippi while he is in custody (Philippians 1.3–7). What would await him in Rome? Should he hope for life or death? He doesn't know

Box 2.3. Paul and slavery

Slavery was normative but largely invisible in the New Testament. The statement of Jesus in Luke 16.13 that the slave cannot serve two masters is proverbial, yet it describes the impossibility of being owned by two people on the assumption that ownership by one person was conventional.

Hellenistic and Roman writers extended Aristotelian notions that slaves are deficient human beings without reason. To Romans, the slave had moral intuition and reason but only for anticipating the owner's wishes. Slaves were often procured through warfare. Freedmen or women as manumitted slaves were nevertheless often bound to a former owner as to a patron.

Paul's letter to Philemon has been commonly understood as a request from Paul to Philemon to take back his runaway slave Onesimus, who had somehow met Paul in prison and been baptized. But Paul does not merely ask Philemon to have pity on Onesimus. Some scholars propose instead that Paul asks Philemon to let Onesimus be apprenticed to him in service of the gospel. In either interpretation, Onesimus is still a thing to be transferred rather than a person to be consulted in the matter.

Slave traders are mentioned in 1 Timothy 1.10. Slaves were employed in households and the economy of the ancient world. In the city of Rome during the first century B.C.E., the number of slaves has been estimated at a third of the total population. In Acts 12.13–16, Rhoda, the slave-girl (*paidiske*), is an example of a 'running slave', a figure in Roman comedy announcing important news. The delivery of this news is delayed and the suspense of the audience builds until it is told.

(Philippians 1.20–22). To be free of life's concerns entirely and serve Christ in Spirit is his desire, and yet he remembers that people like the Philippians need him (1.23–24): 'I am constrained between the two – having the greater and better desire to cast off and be with Christ *and* as more necessary for you to persevere in the flesh.'

The great project of the sacrificial offering of the Gentiles no longer obsessed him. Now only God's kingdom was on his mind, and his body trembled for the Philippians with 'the viscera of Christ'. As he concentrates his own attention, he is concerned that the Philippians should do the same (2.1–2; 4.10), and join their souls with him. And here, in exploring this bodily connection of believers in Christ, Paul makes perhaps his greatest contribution to the movement he had joined his life to, because he shows that Christ as both divine and human is the center of the theology of the Church, superseding any previous revelation, and the center of the emotional commitment of every individual Christian.

After years of saying that various readers should imitate him, just as he imitates Christ, he tells the Philippians what that whole process is about (2.5–8, here given in the King James Version):

> Let this mind be in you, which was also in Christ Jesus: Who, being in the form of God, thought it not robbery to be equal with God: But made himself of no reputation, and took upon him the form of a servant, and was made in the likeness of men: And being found in fashion as a man, he humbled himself, and became obedient unto death, even the death of the cross.

This language is so resonant, it has been described as a hymn – and attributed to a liturgical song that Paul quotes. But even if that is so, Paul is the author who uses this language to speak deliberately of Jesus as God. He has broken through to poetry, and enlists the Philippians in working out the deeply affective salvation that was to be their inheritance by embracing the mind of Christ. Jesus now becomes the focus of faith, because he is divine, and is revealed within the believer so that God's thoughts become human thoughts. 'At the name of Jesus every knee shall bow, in heaven, on earth, and in the underworld' (2.10): Christ receives the honor due God, because he makes humanity divine.

Timothy's edition of Paul
Colossians

In 64 C.E. the Emperor Nero unleashed a pogrom against Christians in Rome, while Paul awaited trial there. The ancient tradition of the Church, that Paul died by beheading at that time, is plausible.

Writing in his own name and Paul's after Paul's death, Timothy sent a letter to Colossae, a city in Asia Minor. It includes reference to Paul's time in Rome (Colossians 4.7–18) and represents the outcome of a visit Timothy must have made there a year or so prior to Paul's death. Colossians includes some of Paul's best poetry, which without Timothy would probably have remained purely oral.

The Christ of Colossians projects his cosmic, divine body into the human experience. The theme of solidarity with this body had long been a theme of Paul's, but in Colossians Christ is the center of the cosmos – natural, social, and supernatural – that created the world and makes the world new each day (Colossians 1.15–20). The range of Paul's thinking was literally cosmic, because the viscera of Christ, the mind of Christ, wove all things into the primordial whole that had been their source. To Paul's mind, the fulfilment of all things had already been accomplished. Christ had mended the world, and an attuned heart and mind could join in that victory.

He still encountered resistance, but he rejoiced in that. He said it was the purpose of the believer to join Christ in suffering (Colossians 1.24), 'to fill up what is lacking in the tribulations of Christ'. Every drop of a martyr's blood flowed from the veins of Jesus, and was shed to reconcile human divisions as decisively as Christ has already reconciled the forces of heaven to the all-consuming love of God. Paul at the end of his life became the first great mystical teacher of union with Christ, the fusion of divine Spirit and human spirit.

Ephesians

Timothy's lasting achievement was to make Paul's poetry available together with the earlier, prose letters to guide a movement passing through its most difficult period. The capstone of his work is probably the letter to the Ephesians. Here the sweeping image of the cosmic Christ in Colossians is used to address the particular tensions between Gentile and Jewish Christians in Ephesus at a later period (Ephesians 2.11–17):

> Therefore remember that you were once Gentiles in flesh, those called foreskin by those called circumcision in flesh – made by hands – because you were in that time apart from Christ, estranged from the citizenship of Israel and foreign to the covenants of the promise, not having hope and godless in the world. But now, in Jesus Christ

Box 2.4. Paul's letters and letters written in his name

Many scholars now accept that not all of the letters attributed to Paul in the New Testament were actually written by him. Rather, one or more of Paul's followers wrote letters in his name.

Letters written by Paul
It is generally accepted that Paul wrote:

- The First Letter to the Thessalonians
- The Letter to the Galatians
- The First Letter to the Corinthians
- The Second Letter to the Corinthians
- The Letter to the Romans
- The Letter to Philemon
- The Letter to the Philippians (with Timothy)

Letters written by Timothy in Paul's name
Paul's follower, Timothy, wrote two letters using his own name and Paul's:

- The Letter to the Colossians
- The Letter to the Ephesians

Letters in Paul's name
Other followers of Paul are thought to have written:

- The First Letter to Timothy
- The Second Letter to Timothy
- The Letter to Titus
- The Second Letter to the Thessalonians
- The Epistle to the Hebrews

you who were once far have become near in the blood of Christ. For he personally is our peace: he made the two one and looses the dividing barrier . . .

Timothy crafted these words for a community in which Gentiles had become dominant, so they would appreciate that it was only God's gracious inclusion of them within Israel that permitted them to inherit the covenantal promise. Christ's aim was to produce 'one new man', joined in 'the body of God' (Ephesians 2.15–16). By the time Ephesians was written, the body of Christ had indeed become the body of God for Pauline Christians, so completely had they incorporated Paul's revelation that Jesus was not only God's Son, but the cosmic reality of divine nature itself.

Letters in Paul's name

When Timothy edited the core of Paul's letters after the apostle's death, adding material of his own, he spurred other Christian writers to continue writing in Paul's name. They produced these new missives as personal letters of Paul to Timothy and Titus, but scholarship is nearly unanimous in rejecting these attributions. In the case of Paul and many other early Christian writers, attributions are not data simply to be accepted or rejected, but indications of the pedigree of the documents concerned. Someone who tried to pass off such works today would be called a forger, but antiquity provides many examples of intellectual enthusiasts who wrote in a great master's name. We only know Socrates' thoughts from Plato's dialogues, and the *Genesis Apocryphon* from Qumran freely embellishes what the patriarchs of Israel said and did. The biblical book of Daniel is pseudepigraphal, written during the second century B.C.E. but attributed to a Jewish sage who lived centuries earlier. Paul had stated openly during his lifetime that he could project his spirit from one place to another (1 Corinthians 5.3–5): he practically invited later disciples to claim his spirit for their own time as well.

1 Timothy, 2 Timothy, Titus

The authors of the letters of 1 Timothy, 2 Timothy and Titus took up this invitation. These writings are often known as the Pastoral Epistles because they deal explicitly with the pastoral imperative to organize, order and care for congregations. In this, their tone and language is unlike Paul's (for example, in Galatians and 1 Corinthians), and also unlike those letters that have come to us in which Timothy had a hand (e.g. Philippians).

Each claims to address Timothy or Titus personally, but the affectionate language of Philemon and Philippians is missing. Timothy

Box 2.5. *Genesis Apocryphon* **from Qumran**

The *Genesis Apocryphon* from Cave one at Qumran (1QapGen) is a narrative of biblical material about Noah and Abraham and Sarah composed in Aramaic that includes embellishments in the first-person singular. Scholars often refer to such material as 'rewritten Scripture' or 'rewritten Bible'.

Column 20 gives an elaborate account of Sarah's beauty: 'How graceful is her breast and how lovely all her whiteness! How beautiful are her arms! And her hands, how perfect!' Pharaoh takes Sarah as his wife but Abraham's life is spared because she identifies him as her brother. Sarah lives with the Pharaoh in Egypt for two years and while there her purity is maintained because God answers Abraham's prayer: 'That night, the God Most High sent him a chastising spirit, to afflict him and all the members of his household . . . and he was unable to approach her, let alone to have sexual intercourse with her, in spite of being with her for two years.'

The *Genesis Apocryphon* illustrates how later authors felt able to imitate original texts. It is authors like these who set the precedent for those who would later write in Paul's name.

and Titus in the Pastoral Epistles are not presented as co-authors with Paul; instead, they receive categorical, often stern advice. These alleged communiqués are unlike Paul's letters to particular churches (or a person, in the case of Philemon). They are rather literary productions that try to crystallize Paul's wisdom for the Church at large.

The Pastorals address the issues of their time, not Paul's. 1 Timothy emphasizes the necessity for prayer on behalf of rulers (1 Timothy 2.1–8), somewhat in the manner of Romans, but against the grain of Paul's proud rejection in Philippians of any citizenship but heaven's (3.20), and is particularly concerned to keep women in their place, which this epistle thinks of as bearing children (1 Timothy 2.13–15):

Because Adam was first fashioned, then Eve. And Adam was not deceived, but the misled woman came into transgression. But she will be saved through childbearing, if they remain in faith and love and sanctification with prudence.

Box 2.6. Paul and women

In contrast to older translations of the Bible, many modern translations recognize women and their roles in early communities. For example, traditional translations such as the Authorized Version (KJV) give Junia's name in Romans 16.7 as a masculine name rather than the feminine form found in the Greek manuscripts. Since Paul identifies Junia as an 'apostle', she provides evidence of women's leadership in the earliest Christian churches.

There is evidence that women did play an important role in Paul's communities. Phoebe, for example, is a patron in a community of Roman believers (Romans 16.1–2). Lydia is a God-fearer and wealthy householder who believed and was baptized by Paul with her whole household. She is patron to both a house church and travelling apostles (Acts 16.11–15).

Another way to approach the topic of Paul and women in the early Church is to focus not on individual women but on the author's arguments about women in general.

In Paul's first letter to Corinth there is an apparent contradiction: while Paul expects women to take an active role in worship in prophetic speech (1 Corinthians 11.5), he also demands women's silence in the assembly at 14.34–35:

> The women should keep silence in the churches. For they are not permitted to speak, but should be subordinate, as the law says. If there is anything they desire to know, let them ask their husbands at home. For it is shameful for a woman to speak in church.

Here we see Paul acting as head of household, preserving order in the community through personal authority in the face of what he understands to be disorderly conduct in Corinth. This is best seen in the fiat of 1 Corinthians 11.16: 'If any man will not be ruled in this question, this is not our way of doing things, and it is not done in the churches of God.' Through ordering and gendering of the household, Paul exercises control over the community, placing special emphasis on particular hairstyles and veiling practices. It is also part of Paul's promotion of an ordered, moderate, upright community that reflects the 'glory' of God – and of Paul.

Thus, female conduct at Corinth or anywhere else is incidental to the main argument establishing Paul's domination and power over those constructed as in need of control. Paul is trying to control women who prophesy, and to limit severely any role they might have in community debate. In the ancient world, prophesying is anarchic and non-gender-specific. Paul intends to counter disorder with an ordered and structured Christian community, in which women 'know their place'. The argument starts with control of his own body (1 Corinthians 7), which is the starting-point for domination of others (1 Corinthians 11). The female body in turn becomes the cultural and rhetorical battleground for the maintenance of custom in Paul. In so ordering the Corinthian 'household', Paul seeks to mirror the stability of an ordered empire. Seen in this light, 1 Corinthians 11.2–16 becomes a powerful statement about Paul's status as head of household and maintainer of Corinthian order. The household is the site of Paul's ability to control, order and dominate.

This becomes the model for the author of 1 Timothy, who writes in Paul's name:

> Let a woman learn in silence with all submission, I permit no woman to teach or to have authority over a man; she is to keep silent. For Adam was formed first, then Eve.
>
> (1 Timothy 2:12–13)

We see again the ideal of restricting women's behaviour in public space. However, this injunction reveals less about women's actual conduct and more about the writer's opinion of women. By means of such texts we can see the ideological uses of interpretation by a male figure in authority to sustain certain relationships of domination.

The proper selection of 'bishops' and 'deacons' (including women) to govern the Church is supposed to assure good order (1 Timothy 3.1–13). Their central authority devolves through 'elders' (both men and women; 1 Timothy 5.1–2, 17–18) and 'widows' (1 Timothy 5.3–16), and the epistle gives instructions (vv. 21–22) about their selection and designation by laying on of hands. All the major terms used in the Pastoral Epistles to speak of offices in the Church had their precedents in the life of the synagogue as well as in Paul's life, but the emphasis on organization and hierarchy is innovative.

In 1 Timothy, enthusiasm for this world and its good order leads to another remark that at first sight looks un-Pauline (1 Timothy 1.8): 'We know that the Law is good, if one makes use of it lawfully.' This is not at all Paul's way of putting the matter, and is enough by itself to endorse the judgment that Paul did not write 1 Timothy. This is a derivative version of the apostle's message for a new and desperate time, after death removed the first generation of the Church's leaders.

The Pastoral Epistles also make Paul speak in a way that serves the interests of hagiography, in presenting Paul as a much more self-confident person than he really was. Who could imagine the author of Galatians or 1 Corinthians or Philippians saying that he served God 'from ancestral origins with clean conscience' (2 Timothy 1.3) – without mention of his career as a persecutor of Christians? And where is Paul's complex relationship with Moses in this unqualified assertion (2 Timothy 3.16): 'All Scripture is God-inspired and useful for teaching, for reproof, for correction, and for training in righteousness'?

Yet that kind of oversimplification pales in comparison to the picture of Paul in the letter to Titus. Here Paul, who seems never to have travelled to Crete, nonetheless leaves Titus there (Titus 1.5), with this warning about the people on the island (Titus 1.12–13): 'One of themselves, their own prophet, said, "Cretans are always liars, evil beasts, lazy-bellies." This testimony is true . . .' Paul was never a diplomat, but for him the coin of insult was sarcasm, not calumny. Those who wrote the Pastoral Epistles did not know him, and used his letters for their own purposes, trimming down more than continuing Paul's thought.

Hebrews

The greatest, most elegant of the post-Pauline epistles is also the last in the present order of the New Testament, and deliberately presents Christian faith as independent of Judaism. Hebrews explains that the Temple on earth (which by this time, 95 C.E., had been destroyed) was only a copy – a shadow of the heavenly sanctuary. Moses had seen the very Throne of God, which was then approximated on earth in the Temple. That approximation is the 'first covenant', and its time has passed. But the heavenly sanctuary offers us a 'new covenant' (9.11–15). Christ entered that true sanctuary in heaven when he died a sacrificial death (9.24) – and its truth, palely reflected in Israel's institutions, is accessible to all who believe in him. Divine vision, the sanctification to stand before God, is in Hebrews the goal of human life, and the only means to such perfection is loyalty to Jesus as the high priest who completes the sacrifice that the practices of Israel could foreshadow but not accomplish.

Jesus is the single focus of revelation in Hebrews, and this Epistle – unlike Paul – relegates Israel to a thing of the past (8.8–13) because the Son's authority is greater even than that of the Scripture. The destruction of the Temple by the Romans shifted the ground of Christian theology: Paul's thought was applied to new circumstances. His vision of the completion of sacrifice in the Temple by means of Jesus' teaching turned into the conviction that Jesus' death had replaced all sacrificial worship.

Many post-Pauline ideas, expressed in letters he did not write himself, continue to be attributed to Paul to this day, making him the apostle many contemporary Christians – and non-Christians – love to hate. Anyone who wants to complain that 'organized religion' has betrayed Jesus can blame Paul the bureaucrat, citing the Pastoral Epistles and Acts. Feminist critics can fasten on that infamous statement in 1 Timothy 2.15 about women overcoming Eve's curse by bearing children. The Paul of Hebrews is an easy target for anyone who is offended by Christianity's claim to supersede Judaism. And who would want to defend what the Paul of the Letter to Titus says about people from Crete?

Paul was nothing like the organizer that Acts and the Pastoral Epistles make him into, but he did want to keep his congregations growing until the final sacrifice on Mount Zion ended the world. His ambivalent attitudes towards women are so confusing that many readers have just written him off as a misogynist, however simplistic that may be. Paul did not think (any more than Jesus did) of Christianity being a separate religion from Judaism, but he relegated the Torah to a position very few of his fellow Jews accepted in his time, and the nearly two millennia since have not changed that.

Paul's ideas remain controversial, disputed to this day. During his life, he found no major community of Christians anywhere that would unequivocally back his position against James or Peter. His greatest letters – to the Galatians, the Corinthians, the Romans, and even to the Philippians – reflect his defensiveness over that simple fact. After his death, even the writings attributed to him often skewed his perspective.

Yet Paul undoubtedly redefined Christianity, shifting the emphasis of Jesus' movement away from realizing the kingdom of God along with Jesus, and towards realizing Jesus himself as the Christ within one's being. Every believer was animated with the Spirit that came from Jesus. Paul claimed to give birth to the divine Son within each believer when they listened to him in faith (Galatians 4.19). Jesus is Christianity's founder, but Paul is its maker – he focused the elements of faith on the formation of the Christ within. That paved the way for what emerged after Paul's death: a faith that survived Nero's pogrom and the Roman burning of the Temple.

Bibliographical background

For a lucid description of the impact of discussion in regard to the relationship of Acts and Paul's letters, see Donald Harman Akenson, *Saint Saul: A Skeleton Key to the Historical Jesus* (Oxford: Oxford University Press, 2000), 134–43. From these considerations, Akenson evolves a chronology comparable to that followed here (144–5), based in its turn on the work of Gerd Lüdemann, *Paul, Apostle to the Gentiles: Studies in Chronology* (tr. F. S. Jones; London: SCM Press, 1984). Lüdemann (99) follows the suggestion of J. B. Lightfoot, originally published in 1865, that Galatians was written later than most scholars place it; see *St. Paul's Epistle to the Galatians* (Peabody: Hendrickson, 1999), 36–56. We follow the view of the majority. All recent discussions of chronology are greatly indebted to Robert Jewett, *Dating Paul's Life* (London: SCM Press, 1979).

The use of Acts in the reconstruction of Paul's development is critically defended by some scholars, such as in Rainer Riesner, *Paul's Early Period: Chronology, Mission Strategy, Theology* (tr. D. Stott; Grand Rapids: Eerdmans, 1998), and vigorously excluded by others; see John Dominic Crossan and Jonathan L. Reed, *In Search of Paul: How Jesus' Apostle Opposed Rome's Empire with God's Kingdom: A New Vision of Paul's Words and World* (New York: HarperSanFrancisco, 2004). The resolution of the question turns on the reasons for which Acts was composed, a topic we turn to in Chapter 4. Most biographers advise critical caution in the use of Acts; see Alan F. Segal, *Paul the Convert: The Apostolate and Apostasy of Saul the Pharisee* (New Haven: Yale University Press, 1990).

Daniel Boyarin succinctly distils a great deal of scholarly discussion in regard to Paul and Stoicism in *A Radical Jew: Paul and the Politics of Identity* (Berkeley: University of California Press, 1994). Jerome Murphy-O'Connor argues that Paul's family had acquired citizenship only during the first century B.C.E., having been enslaved by the Romans in Galilee and exiled to Rome, where his father became a citizen prior to moving to Tarsus; see *Paul: A Critical Life* (Oxford: Clarendon, 1996). A different view, reflected here, is maintained in Bruce Chilton, *Rabbi Paul: An Intellectual Biography* (New York: Doubleday, 2004). Both these biographies deal with Paul's alleged anti-Semitism, and provide bibliographies.

Exercises

1. Paul on women and slavery

Paul's teaching on women and slavery has caused much controversy for later Christians, and he is often quoted in debates about women in the Church today and was appealed to by those who supported slavery. Read the text boxes 'Paul and slavery' on p. 74 and 'Paul and Women' on pp. 80–1, and then answer the following questions.

Questions

1 Identify the women and their roles or offices in Paul's letters and Acts (see Romans 16.1–12; Philippians 4.2–3; 1 Corinthians 1.11; Acts 16.14, 40). What weight do these texts have for modern debates about the roles and offices of women in church or synagogue?

2 Consider how Nympha, head of a house church or assembly (Colossians 4.15), might have heard the words of Colossians 3.18–20:

> Wives, be subject to your husbands, as is fitting in the Lord.
> Husbands, love your wives and never treat them harshly.
> Children, obey your parents in everything, for this is your accept-able duty in the Lord.

3 In a society where slavery was normative, consider how we might understand advice to slaves given in Colossians 3.22–24:

> Slaves, obey your earthly masters in everything, not only while being watched and in order to please them, but wholeheartedly, fearing the Lord. Whatever your task, put yourselves into it, as done for the Lord and not for your masters, since you know that from the Lord you will receive the inheritance as your reward; you serve the Lord Christ.

2. Paul and same-sex relations

The topic of same-sex relations is a vexed one in our day. Only a handful of passages in Paul are cited. According to the Gospels, Jesus is silent on this topic. The passage usually given the most weight is in Paul's letter to the Romans:

> For this reason God gave them up to degrading passions. Their women exchanged natural intercourse for unnatural, and in the same way also the men, giving up natural intercourse with women, were consumed with passion for one another. Men committed shameless acts with men and received in their own persons the due penalty for their error. (Romans 1.26–27)

Paul's teaching in 1 Corinthians is also often cited in the debate:

> Do you not know that wrongdoers will not inherit the kingdom of God? Do not be deceived! Fornicators, idolaters, adulterers,

male prostitutes (Greek: *malakoi*), sodomites (Greek: *arsenokoitai*), thieves, the greedy, drunkards, revilers, robbers – none of these will inherit the kingdom of God. And this is what some of you used to be.   (1 Corinthians 6.9–11)

Questions

1 In Romans 1.26–27:

   (a) Who are the subjects under discussion?
   (b) What does 'for this reason' refer to?
   (c) What kinds of same-sex relations are known in the world of Paul's time? Is this passage about gay men and lesbians? (See Brooten, Gagnon and Via, and Rogers in Further reading.)
   (d) What is 'natural' and what is 'unnatural'? Here, you will want to take into account what Paul's understanding might be both here and in Romans 11.24, and also what the hearers might understand.
   (e) How does this section relate to the rest of the letter to the Romans?

2 The category we know as 'homosexual' did not exist in the ancient world or, indeed, until the nineteenth century. Therefore the Greek words *malakos* and *arsenokoites* cannot mean what we mean by 'homosexuals'. Of course, some behaviour that we today associate with homosexuality may be described in pre-nineteenth-century literature.

   Read the NRSV translation of 1 Corinthians 6.9–11 above, and the section on pp. 10–12 about Bible translations, and then compare this translation of 1 Corinthians 6.9 with others of this passage. For example:

   • The KJV translates: 'Know ye not that the unrighteous shall not inherit the kingdom of God? Be not deceived: neither fornicators, nor idolaters, nor adulterers, nor effeminate [*malakoi*], nor abusers of themselves with mankind [*arsenokoitai*] . . .'.
   • The NIV translates: 'Do you not know that the wicked will not inherit the kingdom of God? Do not be deceived: Neither the sexually immoral nor idolaters nor adulterers nor male prostitutes [*malakoi*] nor homosexual offenders [*arsenokoitai*] . . .'.

- *The Message* paraphrases: 'Unjust people who don't care about God will not be joining in his kingdom. Those who use and abuse each other, use and abuse sex, use and abuse the earth and everything in it, don't qualify as citizens in God's kingdom. A number of you know from experience what I'm talking about, for not so long ago you were on that list.'

Note that the word *malakos* is an adjective and that *arsenokoites* is a noun. The KJV has remained faithful to the parts of speech in the original.

(a) Which translations have remained faithful to the parts of speech in the original?
(b) Do any of the translations include people unidentified in the NRSV?
(c) Can you find other examples of the Greek words *malakos* and *arsenokoites* in other ancient texts? Do they shed any light on meaning here?

Consult, for example, *A Greek–English Lexicon of the New Testament and Other Early Christian Literature* (3rd edn, Chicago: Chicago University Press, 2001), 613b, where the entry for *malakos* is:

(1) Pertaining to being yielding to touch, soft (of things e.g. clothes). Soft clothes or garments are described in Luke 7.35 and Matthew 11.8.
(2) Pertaining to being passive in a same-sex relationship.

3 Look again at 1 Corinthians 1 and 6.9–11. Can you tell which groups of people Paul is writing his letter to?

4. How much weight should Romans 1.26–27 and 1 Corinthians 6.9–11 be given in contemporary discussions of same-sex relations? How do the Greek words *malakos* and *arsenokoites*, which describe two separate groups of persons in 1 Corinthians 6.9, correlate to the modern understanding of gay and lesbian families?

3. Letters in Paul's name

Several of the letters that are traditionally attributed to Paul were probably written by his followers. This was not an uncommon practice in the first century, nor was it done to deliberately deceive. Read the text boxes on the '*Genesis Apocryphon* from Qumran', p. 79, and 'Paul's letters and letters written in his name', p. 77, and then answer the following questions.

Questions

1 Compare the account of Abraham and Sarah in Genesis 12.10–20 with the account in the *Genesis Apocryphon* (see box on p. 79). What purposes might lie behind the *Genesis Apocryphon's* retelling of the story of Abraham and Sarah in Egypt? What is the attitude of the author of the *Genesis Apocryphon* to the text of Genesis?

2 Compare the organizational structure reflected in 1 Corinthians and the Pastoral Epistles (1 and 2 Timothy and Titus). How can you account for the differences?

3 How would you understand and explain the prohibition against women teaching in 1 Timothy 2.12 (written in Paul's name) in the light of Paul's own treatment of women (cf. Romans 16.1–12; Philippians 4.2–3; 1 Corinthians 1.11)?

4. Paul and Jesus

In some scholarly circles it has become fashionable to claim that Paul was the real founder of Christianity, not Jesus: Paul wrote seven of the 27 documents of the New Testament and influenced at least six others; Pauline ideas influenced Augustine and Martin Luther. However, not all scholars agree, and the statement at the end of this chapter, that Jesus is the founder of Christianity and Paul its maker, is an example of one way that the relationship between the two has been defined. Like all such statements by scholars, this is open to evaluation.

Questions

1 How did Jesus see himself? This is sometimes called his 'Messianic self-consciousness'. See, for example, Mark 8.27–35; Mark 10.45.

2 How did Paul see himself? See, for example, 1 Thessalonians 2.7; Galatians 2.11–14; 1 Corinthians 4.15; 2 Corinthians 6.4–10.

3 If Jesus was not the founder of Christianity, what else might he have been?

4 What are the implications of the argument that Jesus was the founder of Christianity?

Further reading

Bernadette Brooten, *Love Between Women: Early Christian Responses to Female Homoeroticism* (Chicago: University of Chicago Press, 1996)

Robert A. Gagnon and Dan Via. *Homosexuality and the Bible: Two Views* (Minneapolis: Fortress Press, 2003)

Deirdre Good, *Jesus' Family Values* (New York: Church Publishing, 2006)

Alison Jasper, *The Shining Garment of the Text: Gendered Readings of John's Prologue*, JSNTSup 165 (Sheffield: Sheffield Academic Press, 1998)

Carolyn Osiek, Margaret Y. MacDonald and Janet H. Tulloch, *A Woman's Place: House Churches in Earliest Christianity* (Minneapolis: Fortress Press, 2005)

Todd Penner and Caroline Vander Stichele, 'Unveiling Paul: Gendering Ethos in 1 Corinthians 11.2–16', *Lectio Difficilior* 2 (2004)

Jack Rogers, *Jesus, the Bible, and Homosexuality: Explode the Myths, Heal the Church* (Louisville, Kentucky: Westminster John Knox, revised expanded edition 2009)

M. B. Skinner, *Sexuality in Greek and Roman Culture* (Oxford: Blackwell, 2005)

3

The Gospels

The Gospels are a unique form of literature, which emerged as a result of Jesus' own teaching and the movement that he inspired. The word in Greek, *euanggelion*, traditionally rendered 'gospel' in English, literally means 'good news', but that translation is too generic to do justice to how this term was used originally. The Greek version of the Scriptures of Israel show that, contextually, the issue was good news in the context of battle, so the word refers to a message or announcement of victory.

In the Aramaic of Jesus' time, *besorta'* – which corresponds to *euanggelion* – referred to such a message of victory. In the book of Isaiah in its Aramaic version (the Targum), for example, the verbal form *basar* is used to speak of the tidings of God's final triumph (Isaiah 52.7), while the noun refers to the message of the prophet who speaks that promise (Isaiah 53.1). These two passages are of especial interest, because they form a precedent for Jesus' preaching. In these quotations, where the Targum introduces new wording as compared to the Hebrew text of Isaiah, italics are used, so that the particular meaning of Isaiah for Aramaic speakers will be clear:

> How beautiful upon the mountains *of the land of Israel* are the feet of him who announces *victory*, who publishes peace, who announces good *victory*, who publishes redemption, who says to *the congregation of* Zion, *The* King*dom of* your God *is revealed.*
>
> (Targum Isaiah 52.7)

> Who has believed *this*, our *message of victory*? And to whom has *the strength of* the *mighty* arm of the Lord been *so* revealed?
>
> (Targum Isaiah 53.1)

Not only do we find here the Aramaic wording (*besorta'* and *basar*) that stands behind 'gospel' (*euanggelion*), and 'preach the gospel' (*euanggelizomai*) in the New Testament, but also the exact equivalent of Jesus' signature concern, the kingdom of God.

Jesus obviously did more than repeat throughout Galilee and Judaea what the Targum of Isaiah already said, but the fact remains that he used the Aramaic language of his time in a way that the Targum helps illuminate. After all, according to Mark's Gospel, Jesus also used the term 'gospel' to speak of news of divine victory, and to refer to his own message, as in the Isaiah Targum. He said both, 'The time has been filled, and the kingdom of God has approached: repent and believe in the message' (Mark 1.15) and, after he was anointed by a woman in Bethany prior to his arrest, 'Wherever the message of victory is announced in the whole world, what she did will also be spoken of in memory of her' (Mark 14.9).

The similarity of usage between Jesus and the Targum indicates that he framed his message in the Aramaic tradition of his own time, and that his usage of the term 'gospel' in particular was shaped by that tradition. His passionate concern was to announce the kingdom of God as the final news of victory, and to call people to belief in that announcement. To do so meant that he crafted oral teaching that his disciples could also convey, and that he also expected his disciples to remember his own story as part of this message. Only on that basis could he expect that what the woman did would 'be spoken of in memory of her'.

This 'gospel' taught by Jesus (usually referred to without capitalizing the first letter) consisted of materials he crafted for memorization, the method by which rabbis taught their disciples. But because he died at an early age for a Rabbinic master, the work of compiling his teaching fell to his successors. His immediate followers were his first successors in teaching, and eventually their numbers included the authors of the texts we call Gospels (with a capitalized first letter), which were written forty years and more after Jesus' death.

Beginning as a prophetic announcement, Jesus' gospel naturally included what he said and did, as in the prophetic books of the Hebrew Bible, and to that extent historical reminiscence is woven into that message. During Jesus' life, the materials concerning him were kept as oral tradition in the memories of his followers. (Literacy rates were low in Antiquity; education in Galilee rarely included reading and writing, and focused on folk memory.) The Gospels in the New

Box 3.1. Good news/gospel

The verb 'to bring good news' (of something to someone) exists in ordinary Greek at the time of the New Testament: in the papyri, for example, Apollonios and Sarapis are thrilled to receive the written announcement from Dionysia of 'the good news of most noble Sarapion's marriage' (Oxyrhynchus Papyrus 3313, second century C.E.). Josephus in Jewish *Antiquities* 5.278, describes the appearance of an angel of God to the wife of Manoch, 'bringing her the good news of the birth of a son (Samson)'. In the Septuagint (the Greek version of the Hebrew Scriptures) the verb refers to oral proclamation. The Psalmist proclaims God's intervention and benefits in Psalm 40.9, 'I have told the good news of deliverance in the great congregation.' So too in Luke 4.18, Jesus applies Isaiah 61.1 to his ministry, 'He has anointed me to announce good news to the poor.'

The neuter plural noun 'good tidings', 'good news' occurs often in Hellenistic proclamations from royalty announcing victories, benefactions or sacrifices celebrated. Matthew 4.23, 'Jesus went throughout Galilee, teaching in their synagogues and proclaiming the good news of the kingdom' (cf. 9.35; 24.14) makes the same connection, attributing royalty to Christ and God but using a neuter singular noun. Use of the neuter singular noun is widespread in the New Testament and seems distinctive among Greek sources. In Aramaic, however, the term *besorta* (the noun equivalent of the verb *basar*) refers to news of victory, including the triumph of God. Paul receives 'good news' as a revelation from God (Galatians 1.11–12; Romans 1.1), which he makes known. Eventually, the term becomes something written: by the third century, the Greek manuscripts identify 'the Gospel according to Mark/Matthew/Luke/John' at the end of the copy.

Testament are the earliest written sources known concerning Jesus, although it is possible (some scholars would say likely) that some of the oral tradition had been preserved in writing prior to Matthew, Mark, Luke and John. Whatever the exact moment at which the transition was made from the oral to the written medium, the Gospels as they can be read today appear to be the result of a cumulative process, involving Jesus' own preaching, the compilation and presentation of his teaching by his disciples, and the writing of the Gospels. Having spoken of Jesus' role in beginning the process of the formation of the Gospels, we will move on in two stages, to the compilations of his disciples, and then to the written Gospels.

Gospels before the Gospels

Peter's teaching

Referring to a visit to Jerusalem in the year 35 C.E., Paul said that he consulted with Peter for 15 days (Galatians 1.18). The purpose of that consultation was for Paul, a new convert to the movement of Jesus, to learn what Peter knew. Peter's gospel is conveyed in those passages in the written Gospels in which Peter is described as being present as a centrally important figure. We can imagine on that basis that the contents would have included, for example, the call of the first disciples, the healing of Jairus' daughter, the confession at Caesarea Philippi, the transfiguration, the Eucharist, and Jesus' struggle in Gethsemane to reconcile himself to the fate of being crucified. As in the cases of all sources in the study of the New Testament and the Hebrew Bible, issues of precise content, dating and origin need to be approached on the basis of inference from the written texts as they stand, and therefore scholars can and do differ in their findings.

The story of the healing of Peter's mother-in-law (Mark 1.29–31; Matthew 8.14–15; Luke 4.38–39) shows that both Peter and his brother had moved to Capernaum, and were living with the family of Peter's wife, a natural arrangement, because the static stock of housing throughout Jewish Galilee meant that marriage often involved men moving in with their in-laws. (Many readers might think it would have been more natural for the woman to leave her family and go to the man's family. But in a subsistence culture such as Jewish Galilee, women normally had no dowry to offer but the roof over their heads.) Jesus was able to establish himself as a rabbi in Capernaum because Simon Peter and Andrew both (see Mark 1.29) received him into their home in Capernaum.

The Gospels portray Jesus as calling Peter and Andrew to become his disciples, along with two other brothers named James and John, while he was walking along the shore of the Sea of Galilee (Mark 1.16–20; Matthew 4.18–22). A vignette that appears in Luke 5.1–11 portrays as present from the outset the dynamic that would mark Jesus' relationship with his prime disciple. Peter is obdurate, and Jesus pushes him. Peter relents, breaks through, shares Jesus' insight, repents and asks forgiveness for his human failures and doubts. Although the descriptions involved are schematic, they give an impression of Peter's character, as well as Jesus'.

The healing of Peter's mother-in-law begins a sequence of passages in which Peter appears to be the origin of an oral source best preserved in Mark, which relates healings of Jesus in which Peter is named as a witness (Mark 1.29–32, 35–45; 5.22–24a, 35–43). An emphasis upon Jesus' healings also characterizes the summary message concerning Jesus' activity attributed to Peter in Acts 10.36–38. Moreover, the words of Peter quoted in the book of Acts identify Jesus as the one whom God 'anointed with Holy Spirit and power' (Acts 10.38), a key theme within the Gospels. Because the forgiveness of sin featured centrally in Jesus' practice of healing as he delivered it to his apostles, the promise of the keys of the kingdom of heaven (Matthew 16.17–19; cf. 18.15–18) is best understood within that context, rather than in the ecclesiastical terms that have mired the saying in controversy in the West regarding papal authority. The time from which Simon would have been called Peter (that is, *Kepha'* in Aramaic) should accordingly be reckoned from when the apostles, with Peter in lead position, were delegated to heal and preach on Jesus' behalf (Mark 3.16; Matthew 10.2; Luke 6.14).

Since the second century c.e., a tradition of the Church has claimed that Mark's Gospel in particular was based on Peter's teaching (see Papias' testimony in Eusebius, *History of the Church* 3.39.15–16). In fact, however, Matthew and Luke also incorporate this material, and these Gospels along with Mark were deeply influenced by Peter.

Box 3.2. Papias and Mark

Eusebius of Caesarea (*c.*263–*c.*339) is often referred to as the Father of Church History because of his work in recording Christianity's earliest years. In his *History of the Church* he records Papias' words about Mark as follows:

> And the presbyter would say this: 'Mark, who had indeed been Peter's interpreter, accurately wrote as much as he remembered, yet not in order, about that which was either said or done by the Lord. For he neither heard the Lord nor followed him, but later, as I said, Peter, who would make the teachings anecdotally but not exactly an arrangement of the Lord's reports, so that Mark did not fail by writing certain things as he recalled. For he had one purpose, not to omit what he heard or falsify them.' Now this is reported by Papias about Mark . . .
>
> (Eusebius, *History of the Church* 3.39.15–16)

'Q'

The Gospels according to Matthew and Luke share a considerable run of material, for the most part sayings of Jesus (amounting to some two hundred verses), which appears to derive from an earlier source. Much of the early work to identify the source was conducted by German scholars, with the result that the source came to be known by the first letter of the German word for 'source', *Quelle*; hence, 'Q'. Because the source can only be identified by a comparison of Matthew and Luke with Mark, rather than by an actual, ancient document, its existence remains a hypothesis, and some scholars deny that it existed.

Recent discussion of 'Q' has brought about a remarkable consensus that at least some of the sayings within it were circulated a few years after the crucifixion, around the year 35 c.e.. The earliest version of 'Q', reflected better in Luke than in Matthew, probably included a charge to Jesus' disciples (Luke 10.3–6, 9–11, 16), a strategy to cope with resistance to their message (Luke 6.27–35), examples of how to speak of the kingdom (Luke 6.20–21; 11.2–4, 14–20; 13.18–21), curses to lay on those who reject those sent in the name of the kingdom (Luke 11.39–48, 52), and a section relating

John the Baptist and Jesus as principal emissaries of the kingdom (Luke 7.24–26, 28, 33–34).

Jesus' teaching was arranged in the form of a memorized message (a mishnah) by his disciples after his death. After the resurrection of Jesus, they continued his activity to Israel at large. Q was preserved orally in Aramaic as the differences in translation in Matthew and Luke sometimes show, and explained how the twelve apostles were to discharge their purpose. It included the materials already mentioned, instructions to Jesus' disciples, a strategy of love to overcome resistance, paradigms to illustrate the kingdom, threats directed towards enemies, and a reference to John the Baptist which would serve as a transition to baptism in the name of Jesus. As specified, that is probably the original order of Q. It is the order that accords with Q's purpose within the redemption of Israel.

One of the themes in the Q tradition concerns the definition of the community of Jesus' followers during his lifetime, in the near future (from the perspective of his followers), and ultimately – the new age that God was about to establish. His followers are portrayed as those who in the present age are deprived and scorned: they are the poor, the hungry, the sorrowing, the hated, the excluded, the reviled (Luke 6.20–22). They are promised a reversal of their condition 'in that day' – that is, the moment when God's purpose is achieved through the Son of Man. Their reward is already stored

Box 3.3. The relationship among Q, Mark, Matthew and Luke

Many scholars believe that Matthew and Luke used the hypothetical document Q as a source as well as the Gospel of Mark when they were writing their Gospels. The relationship between them can be shown in a simple diagram.

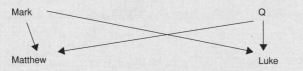

Mark   Q

Matthew   Luke

Figure 2 The relationship between Q, Mark, Matthew and Luke

97

up in heaven in anticipation of that deliverance and vindication. Meanwhile, however, they are to love those who oppose them, to pray for their abusers, to respond generously to those who do them injustice, and to do so in the confidence that God will reward their gracious actions in the new day that is coming (Luke 6.27–36). By refusing to judge others and extending forgiveness to them, disciples will be amply rewarded by God in the future (6.37–42). Since their lives are founded on the compassion of God, they will be able to withstand the difficulties and storms that await them in the future (6.43–49), because divine compassion will be all in all.

Disciples must be prepared, however, for radical conflict with their loved ones, and they must be ready to give up traditional obligations towards the family in view of the higher demands involved in proclaiming the advent of God's kingdom in the near future (Luke 9.57–62). Their commitment to the work of the kingdom will cause violent disruptions in their domestic lives (12.51–53). What is called for in the cause of discipleship is described as hatred towards one's own family and even a willingness to abandon one's own life, as Jesus did in his fidelity to what he believed was God's will for him (14.26–27). There can be no wavering as to where one's ultimate obligations and values are directed: followers must be devoted to God and his work in the world (16.13).

Jesus' followers are to carry forward the work he launched: they must heal the sick and announce the coming of God's rule. To carry out this activity they must move from town to town, indifferent to any conventional system of support, relying only upon the generosity of their hearers, but ready to move on if their message is rejected. Their responsibilities are discharged when they proclaim by word and act the triumphant message of what God is doing through Jesus. God will bring judgment in his own way on those who refuse to heed the message (Luke 10.2–16). The members of the community of Jesus rejoice in the special wisdom about God's purpose that has been disclosed to them through Jesus (10:17, 21–23).

James' teaching

James, the brother of Jesus, became the most influential leader of his brother's movement in Jerusalem. There he was a respected figure in the Temple, acknowledged as a holy man by the population at large, not only by Christians, as Josephus reports (*Antiquities* 20.197–203). James' association with the Temple resulted in his remembering Jesus' last meal with his followers at the time of the meal of Passover, the Seder; James engaged vigorously in framing how followers of Jesus should order their meals, as we know from the book of Acts (Acts 15.19–21). This is the most prominent example of his influence within the Gospels.

Recent scholarship has rightly seen that the identification of Jesus' Last Supper with Passover is theologically motivated. The Gospels correctly report that the authorities had every reason to deal with Jesus *before* the crowds of Passover arrived, and decided that they would act prior to Passover (Matthew 26.1–5; Mark 14.1–2; Luke 22.1–2). Jesus' final meals would therefore have taken place near the paschal season, but not during the actual feast. That would explain why the most basic elements of the Seder – lamb, unleavened bread, bitter herbs (see Exodus 12.1–8) – are notable in the narratives for their absence. Jesus expressed a desire to eat the Passover, as Luke 22.15 indicates, but that desire remained unfulfilled.

Despite these facts, there is no question of any ambiguity in Matthew 26.17–20; Mark 14.12–17; Luke 22.7–14: the passage emphatically presents the Last Supper as a paschal Seder. John's Gospel makes a similar attempt, but with a different timing, making Jesus' death coincide with the *slaying* of the lambs for Passover (John 19.31, 36, with Exodus 12.6, 46). The lambs were slain prior to the meal, so it is clear that the calendar of the early Church (both in James' source and in John's Gospel) has shaped the presentation of events in different but comparable ways.

Timing the Last Supper literally at Passover presents historical problems. Matthew 26.17; Mark 14.12; Luke 22.7 insist that Jesus' instructions to prepare to celebrate the feast in the city were given on the first day of unleavened bread, when the paschal lamb was to be slain. That contradicts the practice mandated in the book of Exodus, where the lamb was to be selected on the tenth day of the month, for slaughter on the fourteenth day of the month (Exodus 12.3–6). Arrangements needed to be made several days prior to the feast for the rule of Exodus to be fulfilled. The scarcity of accommodation in Jerusalem – which is commonly recognized to have had an inadequate infrastructure for the number of pilgrims at

Passover – would have required even more notice. The paradox, then, is that the only passage to insist upon a paschal chronology (see Matthew 26.19; Mark 14.16; Luke 22.13), with the unequivocal reference to the meal as the Passover, does not make good sense in the light of that chronology.

What purpose is served by the strict identification of the Last Supper as a Seder in Matthew 26.17–20; Mark 14.12–17; Luke 22.7–14? Several changes in the understanding of the meal are effected by this liturgical setting, however implausible the precise chronology involved. By means of this tight association with Passover, James inextricably linked Jesus' meal to the liturgical year of Judaism and to Jerusalem. If Jesus' Last Supper were understood as strictly paschal, its re-enactment would be limited in three ways. Temporally, it could only take place at Passover; geographically, the only appropriate venue would be Jerusalem, the only place where paschal lambs could be offered; socially, participants would need to be circumcised (see Exodus 12.48).

The last limitation appears the most dramatic, given the increasing importance of non-Jewish Christians during the course of the first century and later. By fully identifying Jesus' meal and Passover, the circle of potential participants in Eucharist excluded the uncircumcised and was limited to those who were Jews or who accepted circumcision, since circumcision was an explicit requirement for males who took part in a Seder (according to Exodus 12.48–49). Once Jesus' movement reached the Gentiles, the matter of their participation in such a paschal supper would become problematic, if James' teaching were followed. That was exactly what happened when controversy erupted between James and Paul, as we saw in the last chapter.

Mary Magdalene's teaching

Mary Magdalene is the only named recipient of Jesus' exorcism in the New Testament. Moreover, the way in which she is identified (Luke 8.2) – as having been possessed by seven demons – intimates repeated exorcism. Further, every detailed story involving Jesus and unclean spirits bears geographical associations with Mary's native village of Magdala. If we apply the same logic and refer to the same kind of evidence that has been applied to Peter, Mary Magdalene also emerges as the author of a source of stories complete with her oral signature. She was the single most important conduit of stories concerning Jesus' exorcisms.

Simply by following Jesus, the Magdalene evidenced the purifying presence of Spirit; her experience and her standing put her in an ideal position to craft the detailed exorcism stories we read in the Gospels. Read in order in the earliest of the written Gospels (Mark), these three stories amount to a manual of how to cope with unclean spirits (Mark 1.21–28; 5.1–17; 9.14–29): by identifying them, confronting them with divine Spirit, and proclaiming their defeat. They also reflect a progressive development as Jesus honed his craft to deal with increasingly difficult cases of possession.

The first story in the Magdalene source comes from near the beginning of Jesus' time in Capernaum after 24 C.E. (Mark 1.21–28); the second reflects the period of his flight from Herod Antipas in 27 C.E. (Mark 5.1–17); the third appears after Jesus' transfiguration in 31 C.E. (Mark 9.14–29).

The first exorcism story, set in the Capernaum synagogue, depicts unclean spirits whose threat dissolves once they are confronted with purity (Mark 1.21–28). Read in detail, this account clearly reveals Mary Magdalene's oral signature, in terms of geography, method of exorcism, and interest in uncleanness. Her perspective governs the presentation of the story, reflecting an insider's knowledge of the inner struggle that exorcism involved for a person who was possessed.

The demon in the story speaks, but the people in the synagogue hear only inarticulate shrieks. Jesus alone understands the meaning of the sounds. The demon identifies itself with all unclean demons of the spirit world in a fascinating switch of pronouns in the text (here italicized; Mark 1.24): '*We* have nothing for you, Nazarene Jesus! Have you come to destroy *us*? *I* know who you are – the holy one of God!'

The slip back and forth between plural and singular often surprises readers of Mark's text. Multiple demons – like Mary's seven and the demon that found seven colleagues to re-possess a person in one of Jesus' sayings from 'Q' (Luke 11.24–26; Matthew 12.43–45) – signalled the resistance of the demonic world as a whole. Jesus viewed the violence of demons as part of the impending defeat of their regime. In addition to its identification with unclean spirits as a whole, the demon in the synagogue also specifies the purpose of Jesus' exorcisms: not simple banishment, but their definitive removal from power.

Fearing destruction, the unclean spirits act before Jesus speaks, initiating a pre-emptive strike by naming him. Naming was a formula that exorcists usually used to invoke divine power and force demons to obey their commands. Such spells were more effective when they identified a demon by name. In this case, however, the demon jumps in with a spell and a naming of its own. In effect, it is exorcizing the exorcist, a departure from the well-documented form of exorcism stories in the ancient world.

Mary's source describes this as a very noisy event. The demon 'cried out' (Mark 1.23). Jesus shouted back in the rough language of the street, 'Shut up, and get out from him!' (v. 25). The demon's obedience comes under protest; it 'convulsed' its nameless victim and departed with a scream (v. 26).

These acute observations all point towards a storyteller with keen knowledge of the deep combat with evil that Jesus' exorcisms involved, their raucous quality, and the danger that the exorcist would be defeated. Moreover, the storyteller knows how Jesus interpreted the demons' wordless shout (Mark 1.34). Whoever conveyed this story had to know both what went on and what Jesus thought about it. Mary Magdalene best fits the description of that storyteller.

Barnabas' teaching

The prominence of Barnabas within Jesus' movement in Jerusalem has already been seen in Chapter 2; it was Barnabas who introduced Paul to active apostolic work. Barnabas was a Levite, from the priestly caste of Judaism, and had been brought up in Cyprus in a family of wealth. By background, therefore, he brought into Jesus' movement a concern with issues of ritual purity and, at the same time, a positive assessment of the Diaspora. At the same time, he put his wealth at the disposal of the apostles to such an extent that he was known not only as Joseph, his original name, but also by the nickname 'Barnabas', meaning 'son of consolation' in Aramaic (Acts 4.36–37).

The priestly interest in how to maintain true purity in a Diaspora setting, apart from defilement, is reflected in the Gospels. In a famous saying, Jesus said that it is not what goes into a person that defiles, but not by what comes out of a person (Mark 7.15). Jesus' point was that purity comes from the inside out, not the outside in, by what a person does and says, rather than external observance. His original meaning was not limited to food, because a literal restriction to food would have him speaking of regurgitation, rather than ethical behaviour, when he referred to what comes out of a person.

By means of a commentary, however, his teaching was applied to issues of what foods could be eaten even by non-Jews in the Diaspora, far from the original setting of Jesus. In Mark's Gospel, the discussion of Jesus' meaning literally moves to a different place, signalling a fresh setting, and a new meaning is imputed to his words (Mark 7.17–23).

In a house, apart from the crowd, the disciples ask Jesus what he means in his parabolic aphorism concerning what defiles (Mark 7.17). He replies in a way that makes 'what goes into a person' the exact equivalent of food, passing through the stomach and into the latrine, so its risible lack of importance becomes obvious (7.18–19). What proceeds from a person, however, is equated with a list of 'bad thoughts': fornications, thefts, murders, adulteries, covetings, evils, deceit, debauchery, envy, blasphemy, arrogance and foolishness, these are the evils within, which are said to defile a person (7.20–23).

The comment, in response to a question (Mark 7.17–19), specifies that Jesus' original saying had refuted the impurity of foods. The explicit statement at the end of v. 19, 'cleansing all foods', draws out the logic of the comment. The catalogue insists, on the other hand, that defilement is to be taken seriously, once it is understood to be moral instead of alimentary. The list of intellectual vices defines them as the most dangerous, literal impurities. Purity can no longer be a matter of what is eaten, but must be seen as a matter of what is thought.

The wish to transcend concerns about the purity of foods and to emphasize the purity of thoughts is characteristic of Hellenistic Christianity. Paul reports (with favor) on the practice in Antioch before emissaries from James came, when meals could be conducted with common fellowship among Jewish and non-Jewish followers of Jesus (see Galatians 2.12). The tendency of Hellenistic communities of Christians to mix their Jewish and non-Jewish constituencies, and therefore to relax or ignore issues of purity in foods, is here documented by Paul (*c.*53 C.E.). The vocabulary of the list of vices in Mark 7 is also more typical of the Pauline literature (in the broad sense) than of any other body of literature in the New Testament. Such vices are classed as impurity in Romans 1.24; Galatians 5.19; Ephesians 4.19; 5.3; Colossians 3.5. Early Christianity (which Pauline literature reflects) saw a shift in the understanding of the medium of impurity: no longer foods, but moral intentions, conveyed the danger of defilement.

Paul seems to dismiss the conception of purity itself; the logical extension of his analysis is that all things are pure to the pure (so Titus 1.15). The circle responsible for Mark 7.20–23, on the other hand, insists upon the danger of impurity but sees the contagion in moral terms. The identification of the circle is obviously a matter of inference, but – among the possibilities given by Paul in Galatians 2 – the most plausible is that of Barnabas. In effect, once Jesus enters the house in Mark 7.17, a new social setting is addressed, and the point of his teaching, as commented upon and expanded by means of a catalogue, is that vices rather than foods are sources of impurity.

Other sources behind the written Gospels have also been identified, and the identification of any source involves inference, but those we have discussed are often referred to by commentators. By taking account of how teaching evolved among Jesus' followers, we can better appreciate the richness and variety of the written Gospels.

Written Gospels

The first three Gospels in the New Testament, Matthew, Mark and Luke, follow the common structure of Peter's teaching, as described above. Each of them is distinctive, but their common order means that they are 'synoptic': they can be seen together by printing them in parallel columns. A book which lays the Gospels out that way is called a Synopsis, and the first three Gospels are called the Synoptic Gospels. They are the first of the written Gospels, and are followed by John in the New Testament. We will consider these Gospels in their chronological order, and then turn to the Gospel according to Thomas, the most famous of the Gnostic Gospels from the second century.

No Gospel is simply a copy of another; rather, each represents the choices among varying traditions, written and/or oral, and the development of those traditions that had taken place in a given locality. Although a consensus is emerging in regard to the cities in which each Gospel emerged, a consensus reflected here, their origins are a matter of inference, based upon clues in the texts themselves and later traditions of the Church. Similarly, the actual authors of each Gospel are unknown. Who they were, where they worked, and what the purpose of their writing was, are all matters that must be inferred from the texts themselves.

Box 3.4. Gospel beginnings

All beginnings are important. Each of the Gospels has a different opening that sets the stage for what follows.

The opening of Mark is a continuous flow of words blending the Gospel writer's narrative with words of the prophet and words of God. There is no break between what is written in Isaiah and what the narrator and God say. The small Greek word *kai*, translated 'and' or 'now', and sometimes 'but', strings the narrative together: 'and preaching a baptism of repentance' (v. 4), 'and all the country of Judaea went out to him and all the inhabitants of Jerusalem and they were baptized by him . . . Now John was clothed . . . and he wore a leather belt . . . and was eating locusts and wild honey [vv. 5–6] and he preached . . .' (v. 7).

Matthew's opening seems to be alluding to Genesis 5.1, 'This is the book of the generations . . .'. The Gospel continues with a genealogy that follows a set pattern, 'X begat Y', echoing the genealogies of Genesis 5.

Luke's literary introduction, or Preface, differs from the beginnings of Mark and Matthew (Luke 1.1–4). It identifies an author, explains his intention, and refers to contemporary writings that, like his, report what has happened recently.

If we examine these Gospel openings carefully we will see clues as to what to expect in the rest of the Gospel and consequently read what follows differently.

Mark

The Gospel 'according to Mark' (its title in antiquity) appears to be the oldest of the Gospels, since its material is almost wholly replicated in the Gospels according to Matthew and Luke. As we have seen, Papias of Hierapolis in Asia Minor claimed during the second century that Mark had been the interpreter of Peter, and wrote down what Peter recalled that Jesus said or did. The writing that now bears Mark's name seems to have been compiled from oral and written sources that consisted of relatively short runs of tradition from several informants. This Gospel does not have the strict narrative sequence one might expect from a report from a firsthand observer. The baptism of Jesus must have come early in the development of his public persona, and the confrontation with the authorities in Jerusalem obviously came at the end of his career; otherwise there is little firm indication of chronological order in the Gospel according to Mark. Mark does not read as a biography would, but was written with the significance of Jesus in mind: declared God's Son at his baptism (1.11), made known as such to his most privileged followers (9.7), as well as to a Roman centurion at the moment of the crucifixion (15.39).

The sources most immediately used by the author were apparently Greek, since quotations from the Scriptures are for the most part based on Greek, rather than Hebrew, originals. Still, from time to time Aramaic in sayings of Jesus is directly transliterated, and the version of Isaiah he cites agrees in crucial cases with the Targum (the Aramaic version) of Isaiah. For example, the final verse of the book of Isaiah in the Targum identifies who will suffer – and specifies where they will suffer – at the end of time, when it adds to the Hebrew reading (with the addition italicized here), '*the wicked* shall be *judged in Gehenna until the righteous will say concerning them, We have seen enough*' (66.24). 'Gehenna' is just what Jesus associates with the statement that 'their worm will not die and their fire will not be quenched' (Mark 9.48, and see vv. 44, 46 in many manuscripts), which is taken from the same verse of Isaiah.

That would suggest that, although some of Mark's sources ultimately reached back to Jesus and his immediate followers, they had already been rendered into Greek by the time the Gospel was composed. Mark's language is a rough-and-ready Greek, with occasional hints that Aramaic locutions have influenced the style. Yet some of the terms used are derived from Latin as well.

Mark must have been written in a place where Greek was the common language, where there was exposure to Roman culture, and yet where part of the underlying culture was Semitic-speaking. Papias referred to Rome as the city of origin, and a large Jewish commun-ity had existed there since the second century B.C.E.. The importance for Mark of Jesus' challenges to Jewish leaders – priests, Sadducees and Pharisees – suggests that it was written with some awareness of these groups and their influence. At the same time, Mark's grasp of the basics of Judaism is sometimes tenuous at best (see Mark 7.3–4). The same paradox of local knowledge expressed side by side with surprising ignorance emerges in the special attention paid in Mark's narrative to the Gentile cities Tyre and Sidon and to the distant but also Gentile Decapolis, which in Mark's occasionally bizarre geography are spoken of as if they were in proximity to one another (Mark 7.31). As a whole, Rome would seem to be this Gospel's city of origin, because it maintained sufficient contact with Judaism and Jerusalem to explain Mark's high level of information, but was also sufficiently distant from them (sometimes to the point of anti-Semitism) to explain Mark's lapses into implausibility and geographical ignorance.

The most extensive passage in Mark that treats a unified theme is Mark 13, often referred to as 'the Markan apocalypse', and which directly concerns any effort to date the composition of the Gospel. It portrays the end of the age, the sufferings of the faithful and the destruction of the Temple. The links between this part of Mark and the book of Daniel reinforce the impression that this final discourse of Jesus in Mark is apocalyptic by intent.

The seers of the apocalyptic tradition conveyed (1) a way of understanding history, (2) a belief about how knowledge of God's purpose is communicated to human beings, and (3) a set of assumptions about the community that is the recipient of this knowledge, including their immediate prospects of struggle and suffering and their long-range confidence in divine vindication. In this view of the world, history is the story of the conflict between divine forces and the forces of evil, which for the time being have seized control of the human situation, subjecting both political powers and individuals to demonic control. God has disclosed to the faithful that they will have to endure suffering, even martyrdom, for some time to come, but that through his chosen agent, the hostile forces will be overcome and the divine rule established. In that new situation, the faithful will share in the rule of God and will be fully vindicated in the triumph over evil. This knowledge cannot be inferred from the course of events or arrived at by human wisdom, according to the perspective of apocalypse, but is given in veiled form only to the elect community. This outlook on God, the world and the community of faith pervades the Gospel according to Mark.

Mark's specific concern in chapter 13 with the threatened coming of armies to seize Jerusalem and destroy the Temple may make it appear to date from the years after the priestly nationalists began their revolt against the Romans but before the Temple was destroyed: that is, between 66 and 70 c.e.. On the other hand, Mark's emphasis upon the comprehensive defeat of Jerusalem and the destruction of the Temple suggests that a date after the Roman campaign (*c.*73 c.e.) is more plausible.

Matthew

The Gospel 'according to Matthew' (its title in antiquity) owes its position as the first book in the New Testament to its widespread usage in the ancient Church, as is shown by frequent references to this Gospel among the Fathers of the Church and within Gnostic writings. The Gospel owes its title to its identification of a tax agent and disciple by that name (Matthew 9.9), although he is called Levi in Mark (2.14) and Luke (5.27). Yet the name 'Matthew' does appear in all three Synoptic Gospels as among the Twelve (Matthew 10.3; Mark 3.18; Luke 6.15): the first Gospel's innovation lies not in the name, but in its association of that name with the disciple who was or had been a tax agent.

The first Gospel shows a keen interest in how Jesus' life and work fulfils prophecies in the Scriptures of Israel, in the final judgment which is to accompany the end of the world, in the teaching of angelology, and in the emerging custom of celibacy among believers (Matthew 19.1–12). All of these features suggest a Syrian provenance, and particularly from Damascus (although Antioch has also been suggested), where there were disciples of Jesus from shortly after the resurrection, and where Jewish communities thrived. Among them, the Essenes also featured prominently, and some distinguishing characteristics of Matthew's Gospel, especially its presentation of Jesus as the authoritative teacher of the Law, echo features of the Dead Sea Scrolls, where the figure called the Teacher of Righteousness is also portrayed in Mosaic terms.

Chapter 23 of the Gospel nonetheless reflects the growing tension with many Jewish communities that did not recognize Jesus as Son of God and messiah, as well as the growing importance of the institution of the synagogue in the period after 70 C.E., when the Romans destroyed the Temple. The Roman arson of Jerusalem finds its allusion in Matthew 22.7. That reference, together with the evidence of the growing power of the Pharisees and the influence of synagogues, has suggested to scholars that the Gospel should be dated around 80 C.E..

Considerable overlap with the Gospel according to Mark has led many scholars to suppose that Mark constituted a source of Matthew, but the shared material need not all have been in written form, since oral instruction was vital within the primitive Church. Similarly, the presence of some 200 verses, for the most part sayings of Jesus, in both Matthew and Luke has prompted the hypothesis of a *written* document called 'Q', but sayings need have been no more formalized in writing than the teachings of Peter, James and Barnabas, which also seem to have influenced the composition of Matthew.

But the first Gospel is no mere patchwork of sources. Its structure is clearly marked through its preface, a unique presentation of Jesus' birth from the perspective of scriptural fulfilment (chapters 1–2), and through clearly marked sections that tie together narrative and discourse (including the famous and uniquely Matthaean Sermon on the Mount) as Jesus progresses from his baptism and preaching in Galilee (chapters 3–4), through his healings, both personally and by means of the Twelve (chapters 8–10), into an emphasis upon his own persona (chapters 11–13), until he explicitly proclaims his authority to his followers (chapters 14–17), clashes with the authorities in Jerusalem (chapters 19–25), and passes through death to resurrection (chapters 26–28).

The fivefold structure of the middle section recalls the five books of Moses. This impression is strengthened by the explicit contrast between Jesus' rules for his people and those given by Moses in the first discourse (Matthew 5.21, 27, 31, 33, 38, 43). Just as Moses went up on the mountain to give instruction to God's people (Exodus 24), so Jesus repeatedly in Matthew ascends a mountain to inform God's people and to manifest his divine authority (Matthew 4.8; 5.1; 14.23; 15.29; 17.1; 28.16). In Jesus' presentation of his people's responsibility to God in this Gospel there is a distinctive emphasis on true righteousness, in contrast to that of the Pharisaic tradition (3.15; 5.6, 10, 20; 6.1, 33). That theme is most fully developed in a discourse of chapter 23, which evolved as the hostility between Matthew's community and the Pharisees (or rabbis as Matthew already begins to call them) intensified. This hostility comes to its most radical expression when the Jewish people willingly call down responsibility for shedding Jesus' blood on themselves *and their children*, and this after Pilate – the only person with authority to order the execution – has washed his hands of guilt (Matthew 27.24–25). The climax of the Gospel is reached at the close, when the eleven dis-ciples (after Judas delivered Jesus to the authorities and then killed himself) are commanded to make disciples of all nations by baptism 'in the name of the Father and of the Son and of the Holy Spirit', and by teaching them to keep Jesus' commandments (28.19–20).

Luke

The Gospel 'according to Luke' (its title in antiquity) and 'Acts', now separated in the Christian canon of Scripture by the Gospel according to John, were composed as a two-volume work, which begins with the divine preparation for the birth of Jesus and ends with Paul in Rome, symbolizing the worldwide mission of the Church. The similar opening lines of each, the dedication to the same person (named as Theophilus), and the reference in Acts 1.1 back to 'the earlier book' all indicate a common author. The similarity in editorial style and overall point of view confirms this conclusion, which is taken for granted by scholars across the spectrum of stances.

Since the second century and to the present, the author has been identified as the Luke who is mentioned as a co-worker of Paul in Philemon 24 and 2 Timothy 4.11 and described as a 'beloved physi-cian' in Colossians 4.14. Some scholars have inferred from the occa-sional shifts in the narrative of Acts from 'they' to 'we' (see, for example, Acts 16.1 with 16.11; 20.1 with 20.6) that the author was a companion of Paul on part of his journeys around the Mediterranean Sea. But the change from third person to first person plural is found in historical writings of the period, and in any case appears in con-nection with Timothy in Acts, rather than Luke. More likely, the author, as he states openly in Luke 1.1–2, was not himself an eyewit-ness of the events he reports, but based his account on reports he had heard or read from those who were. For convenience, we refer to him as Luke, but as is the case with the other Gospels, the identity of the authors is simply unknown, and probably has been from the earliest years of the document's existence, and many sources – oral and written – fed into the final product.

The final author is nonetheless remarkably skilled and fluent as a writer. This is apparent in the ability to modify the Gospel's style in ways that are appropriate to the material presented. In the opening section of the Gospel (Luke 1—3), for example, the writ-ing sounds 'like the Bible' – that is, it effectively mimics the style of the Septuagint (which was, of course, the version of the Bible that Luke was using) and gives the reader a sense of continuity between the characters from biblical history and the events the Gospel recounts. Some of these connections are implicit, such as the parallels between the divine gift of a son, John, to the childless couple Zechariah and Elizabeth (1.5–25, 57–80) and the story of the birth of Samuel in 1 Samuel 1. The exultant hymns that celeb-rate these miraculous births are also similar (cf. 1 Samuel 2 and Luke 1.67–79). Other connections are explicit, such as the angelic voice that links the birth of Jesus to the divine assurance to David that he will have an enduring royal line (2.10–11). The care with which the ritual requirements are fulfilled for both the boys and the testimony of the pious men and women around the Temple strengthen this sense of continuity within the history of God's cov-enant people. Luke's depiction of the new community's outreach to the humble and to outsiders is anticipated in the coming of the shepherds at Jesus' birth (Luke 2.8–20).

Box 3.5. Septuagint

The Greek version of the Hebrew Bible became a sacred text (Scripture) for Greek-speaking Jews in the Diaspora who no longer spoke Hebrew. Together with the Greek New Testament, it became the Bible of early followers of Jesus. The Letter of Aristeas explains the origins of a Greek translation of the five books of Moses probably in mid-third-century B.C.E. Alexandria, where a Greek-speaking Jewish population already existed. This translation is often known as the LXX (70), after the alleged number of translators.

Although the third Gospel relied on Mark, or Mark-like tradition, as well as on Q as its basic sources, Luke adapts them to its own purposes, rearranging the sequence and adjusting the details. In various editorial additions the final writer shows familiarity with literary conventions of the period, such as the dating of events by reference to several concurrent rulers (Luke 3.1–2) and the composition of extended speeches by leading characters in his story. In the overall narrative of Acts, where we learn how the gospel moved from Jerusalem to Rome, the style resembles that of a popular literary genre of the second century C.E. and later, known as the romance.

The major objective of Luke in both volumes of this work (Luke and Acts) is to show that from the beginning, the covenant people of God have had the divinely intended potential to become a universally inclusive community. Both volumes acknowledge that not all will be persuaded by God's message through Jesus, but everyone has the possibility of responding in faith to this gospel. For example, when Simeon blesses the child Jesus in the Temple (Luke 2.28–32), he declares that Jesus' coming is intended as 'a light to reveal your will to the Gentiles, and to bring glory to your people Israel'. Similarly, in the extended quotation from Isaiah at Jesus' baptism, we read, 'All flesh will see God's salvation' (Luke 3.4–6; cf. Mark 1.3). That aim is apparent in the special material that Luke has included, as well as in the modification of sayings and narrat-ives taken over from earlier sources. In its portrayal of a universalizing Christianity and its access to widespread traditions concerning Jesus in both Aramaic and Greek, Luke's Gospel probably derives from Antioch around the year 90 C.E..

John

The Gospel 'according to John' (its title in antiquity) is widely recognized as the last in the New Testament to have been written, around 100 C.E. in Ephesus. Although we do not know who wrote this anonymous work, frequent references to the disciple whom Jesus loved (13.23–25; 19.26–27; 20.2–8; 21.7, 20), and his identification as the one who remembered or recorded this Jesus material, led many in the early Church to the conclusion that the Gospel was written by John, the son of Zebedee, although he is never mentioned by name in the Gospel. The reference in 21.22 to the possibility that this disciple might live until Jesus returned to earth led some to suppose that he was writing at a greatly advanced age, perhaps late in the first century. No matter how appealing, these are no more than ancient guesses, and in any case the Gospel itself refers to a group of people who received the testimony of the beloved disciple and wrote the words of the text (21.24).

What is clear is that this Gospel is not directly dependent on the other Gospels and that its composers and writers were more interested in symbolic meaning than in historical narrative. Indeed, John shows delight in using words with double meaning – for example, Jesus in John says to Nicodemus in Greek that one must be born *anothen* in order to see the kingdom of God (John 3.4). The term can mean either 'from above' or 'again', and the passage goes on to explore Nicodemus' misunderstanding, so that the audience will grasp both meanings rather than choose between them.

Two major cultural factors influenced the reworking of traditions in John. The first derives from the wisdom tradition of the Hellenistic age as developed in Judaism. Wisdom had been understood since the time of Proverbs 8 as the dimension of God by which he created all things, and discloses himself to humanity. The second is manifest in the keen interest among both Jews and Gentiles of the first century C.E. in forms of religion that offered the possibility of a direct experience of God, especially through visions and hearing sacred messages. With a growing sense of the vast difference between God and human beings came a yearning for some

113

instrument or agent by which mere humans could benefit from contact with the sovereign, holy God. For some, this mediating agency was found in Wisdom, viewed as the first of God's creations and even as his co-creator (Proverbs 8) and as the channel through which know-ledge of God comes to human beings. Others hoped for a direct vision of God, on the model of the experiences of Moses, Elijah, Ezekiel and Daniel, whose very appearance was altered as a consequence of their having contacted God. In the Gentile world of this time, there was a similar striving for religious experiences that would bring together the hallowed traditions of divine wisdom with a direct and immediate experience of the deities.

The prologue to the Gospel according to John (1.1–16) speaks of the 'Word', or *logos*, of God as the instrument of creation and of divine self-disclosure. In a way that recalls the roles of Wisdom, but at the same time is significantly different because it is identified with a particular person, the Word enables human beings to become members of God's own people (1.12–13). This admission to the new community of faith differs completely from natural birth into an ordinary human family or race. Indeed, the Word's own people did not receive him (1.11). This unique Son of God is the source of the light of the knowledge of God (1.4) and of the radiance of God's glory (in contrast to the Temple, where God's glory once shone) and is the channel of God's grace and truth (1.14, 16, 18). The requirement for becoming God's child is to trust God's Son (1.12). John the Baptist prepared for Jesus' coming (1.6–9, 19–27), denying that he was himself the Light, and acclaiming Jesus of Nazareth as the Lamb of God, who takes away the world's sin (1.29, 36), and as the Spirit-anointed Son of God (1.32–34). At the outset of his public career, Jesus begins to rally around him the core of his followers, who acclaim him as Messiah, Son of God, and King of Israel (1.41, 49). He responds by promising them that they will see his ultimate vindication by God's angels as Son of Man (1.51). Paradoxically, John's Gospel pictures Jesus as fully human ('son of Joseph'; 1.45) but also as sharing the nature of God (1.18; 8.58; 17.21).

The *Gospel according to Thomas*

This Gospel, an anthology of Jesus' aphorisms and parables, was compiled during the second century, too late to be included in the New

Testament, but early enough to make it of great interest to the study of Jesus and early Christianity. In addition, *Thomas* is a principal and early representative of a powerful religious impulse that rippled through the Roman empire between the late first century and the end of the fourth century C.E.. Gnosticism sought for a single, integrating insight into the divine world amid the conflicting religious traditions of the ancient world. Gnostics wanted direct contact with the divine apart from parochial requirements, peculiar customs and ethnic preferences. Traditional religions talked about transcendence, but they restricted the delivery of their truths to their different constituencies, which were limited and often mutually exclusive, defined by race, history, family or status. Gnosticism claimed to smash through those barriers, making it the most potent cultural force in this period of the Roman empire and one of the most successful efforts at the intellectual reform of religion there has ever been.

Thomas was first compiled in the Syriac language in the ancient city of Edessa in Syria. But Gnosticism was an international movement, and *Thomas* was also embraced in Egypt and translated into Coptic, the first-century inheritor of the language of the hieroglyphics. The Coptic language itself is key to Gnosticism's success in Egypt. The hieroglyphics of ancient Egypt were difficult to write and read, but Coptic put that language into the phonetic system of the Greek alphabet (with four extra characters). That innovation enabled people with leisure in rural Egypt to read and hear recitations of the world's wisdom in their own tongue. They became avid for philosophy, religion and esoteric knowledge, and Gnosticism packaged them all in a way that assured its advance on Egyptian soil. The earliest complete copies of Thomas, from the fourth century C.E., were discovered in 1945, in a library of Gnostic writings discovered near Nag Hammadi.

In Thomas, the 'Living Jesus' – the eternal personality whom death could not contain – speaks wisdom that promises immortality. The Coptic text includes material presented in the canonical Gospels as well as teaching culled from oral traditions. *Thomas* focuses so completely on the wisdom spoken by the Living Jesus in response to questions from his disciples that it does not include any stories about Jesus. As the Living Jesus responds to his disciples' problems, doubts and entreaties, his epigrammatic wisdom becomes a rich, rhythmic chant – a guide for Gnostic meditation complete with oral cues.

Many images and parables familiar from the New Testament Gospels appear in Thomas as well. Examples include the parable of the sower and the seed (9), the mustard seed (20), the city on a hill (32), a seed (57), the feast (64), the pearl (76), the tenant farmers (65), the persecuted and hated are blessed (68), the harvest and labourers (73), foxes and holes (86). Many sayings are unique to Thomas in form and content. One of the most famous of them is probably authentic: 'Who is near to me is near the fire; who is far from me is far from the kingdom' (87). Many other sayings are outwardly similar to those in the canonical Gospels but differ significantly in meaning. For example, the need to become as a child in order to enter the kingdom is not a call for simple trusting acceptance, as in Mark (10.15), but a demand to transcend one's sexual identity (*Thomas* 22, 37). This is an important feature of the overall emphasis in *Thomas* on achieving *unity*, which is variously described as being solitary (75) or as two becoming one (11, 16, 61, 75, 106). This means that the divided nature of human existence (body and soul, flesh and spirit, male and female) is overcome and surpassed as one enters a new realm of spiritual unity. This is a basic concept of Gnosticism, which commonly regarded the material world, including bodily existence, as inherently evil. Through the disclosure of divine knowledge that God provides through Jesus the ultimate individual unity is attained. Anyone who gains this status is free of human limitations and liberated from the body, which Thomas regards as a corpse (15, 60, 71, 80, 111).

These insights are gained only through the divine knowledge that God has provided, which includes true knowledge of the self (3, 5, 6, 13, 17, 18). Divine knowledge exists as inner light (24, 70) and is already within the elect individuals, waiting to be recognized (61, 62, 70). It is through Jesus that this divine awareness comes (77, 108): he enables men and women to overcome their sexual separateness and thus to achieve divine androgyny (114). Those who receive this new knowledge will be free from the body and its enticements (27, 28, 56, 87) and will become detached observers of the passing world (42). Redemptive significance is not attached to the death of Jesus in this Gospel, which is mentioned as only an instance of spirit triumphing over the body. There are no references to the sacraments and no mention of covenant or community responsibilities, either within the group or towards outsiders or towards the state.

The Gnostics who lived near Nag Hammadi in Egypt, away from cities in their rural enclaves, used the *Gospel according to Thomas* as well as other texts deposited there to deepen their *gnosis* (knowledge). *Thomas* clearly states its purpose, and the aim of Gnosticism as a whole: 'The one who finds the interpretation of these sayings will not taste death' (saying 1). *Thomas* promises to convey the reality of resurrection to the attentive Gnostic, whose goal is to cheat death itself. *Thomas* represents no single source of Jesus' teaching, but like John it shows that the genre of instruction proved to be a useful vehicle of theological reflection long after the time of 'Q'.

We are presented in our principal sources (the Gospels of the New Testament and *Thomas*) with ways of seeing Jesus within the communities that each Gospel was intended for. Identifying the view of Jesus each one takes, we can infer how Jesus must have acted to produce that view of him, together with the distinct views of him the other sources take. We are dealing, not only with four or five documents, Matthew, Mark, Luke, John and *Thomas*, but also with the groups of followers of Jesus that produced materials for those documents. These writings are so distinctive that the term 'gospel', originally an Aramaic term for a prophetic announcement of God's victory, came to be applied to them as an appropriate title – and a new genre of literature.

Bibliographical background

Study of the genre of the Gospels, as compared to Graeco-Roman literature, has been a thriving topic, bringing varying estimates of the historical element in the Gospels; see Charles H. Talbert, *What is a Gospel? The Genre of the Canonical Gospels* (Philadelphia: Fortress Press, 1977); Adela Yarbro Collins, *Is Mark's Gospel a Life of Jesus? The Question of Genre* (Milwaukee: Marquette University Press, 1990); Lawrence M. Wills, *The Quest of the Historical Gospel: Mark, John and the Origins of the Gospel Genre* (London: Routledge,

1997); Michael E. Vines, *The Problem of Markan Genre: The Gospel of Mark and the Jewish Novel* (Leiden: Brill, 2002).

As that work has proceeded, scholars have also pursued the question of how Jesus' followers shaped traditions they had received into sources, which in turn influenced the Gospels in terms of shape as well as content. Among them, prominent contributions include Wilfred L. Knox, *The Sources of the Synoptic Gospels* (Cambridge: Cambridge University Press, 1953); Birger Gerhardsson, *Memory and Manuscript: Oral Tradition and Written Transmission in Rabbinic Judaism and Early Christianity*, Acta Seminarii Neotestamentici Upsaliensis 22 (tr. Eric J. Sharpe; Lund: C. W. K. Gleerup, 1961); Thorleif Boman, *Die Jesus-Überlieferung im Lichte der neueren Volkskunde* (Göttingen: Vandenhoeck & Ruprecht, 1967); Étienne Trocmé, *Jesus as Seen by His Contemporaries* (Philadelphia: Westminster, 1973); Bo Reicke, *The Roots of the Synoptic Gospels* (Philadelphia: Fortress Press, 1986); Maurice Casey, *Aramaic Sources of Mark's Gospel* (Cambridge: Cambridge University Press, 1998) and *An Aramaic Approach to Q: Sources for the Gospels of Matthew and Luke* (Cambridge: Cambridge University Press, 2002); James D. G. Dunn, *Jesus Remembered: Christianity in the Making* 1 (Grand Rapids: Eerdmans, 2003); Richard Bauckham, *Jesus and the Eyewitnesses: The Gospels as Eyewitness Testimony* (Grand Rapids: Eerdmans, 2006).

As opposed to these approaches, a vigorous argument has been mounted that the Gospels are best explained in strictly literary terms by one author using the work of another. See William R. Farmer, *The Synoptic Problem: A Critical Analysis* (New York: Macmillan, 1964); David L. Dungan, *A History of the Synoptic Problem: The Canon, the Text, the Composition, and the Interpretation of the Gospels* (New York: Doubleday, 1999). In developing our approach, we have been guided by the classic work of Burnett Hillman Streeter, *The Four Gospels: A Study of Origins, Treating of the Manuscript Tradition, Sources, Authorship, and Dates* (London: Macmillan, 1930).

Exercises

1. Three different Gospel openings

Matthew, Mark and Luke each gave their Gospels distinctive openings which set their agenda for the rest of their Gospel. Read the

Box 3.6. Gnosticism and the *Gospel of Thomas*

This chapter interprets the *Gospel of Thomas* from the perspective of the emergence of Gnosticism. Other scholars propose that *Thomas* is actually an early Christian Wisdom text because none of its 114 sayings explicitly describes a systematic pattern of Gnostic thought. Whether such a system of thought is presumed in *Thomas* remains a matter of debate. While the text of Thomas exists in a fourth-century Coptic version, there are earlier second- and third-century Greek fragments from Oxyrhynchus (P.Oxy.1, 654 and 655) to which the Coptic text is related, and both the Coptic and the Greek versions may go back to an original in Syriac.

The following sayings from *Thomas* will give you a flavour of the text and help you to make up your own mind.

The *Gospel of Thomas* opens thus (saying 1):

> These are the secret sayings which the living Jesus spoke and which Judas Didymos Thomas wrote down. And he says, 'Whoever discovers the interpretation of these sayings will not experience death.'

Since the opening identifies 'secret sayings' that Jesus spoke, scholars have identified *Thomas* as an example of collected sayings. Such collections exist in antiquity and in modern times; they exist to be studied and memorized as thoughts of wise people. Because the sayings of *Thomas* are secret, they require investigation. They indicate knowledge of an immediate living Jesus. Such scrutiny promises wisdom and immortality.

In this text it is the disciple Thomas who transmits Jesus' sayings, which is why he features in saying 13:

> Jesus says to his disciples: 'Compare me, tell me whom I am like.' Simon Peter said to him: 'You are like a just messenger.' Matthew said to him: 'You are like a (especially) wise philosopher.' Thomas said to him, 'Teacher, my mouth will not bear at all to say whom you are like.' Jesus says: 'I am not your teacher. For you have drunk, you have become intoxicated at the bubbling spring that I have measured out.' And he took him, (and) withdrew, (and) he said three words to him. But

> when Thomas came back to his companions, they asked him:
> 'What did Jesus say to you?' Thomas said to them: 'If I tell
> you one of the words he said to me, you will pick up stones
> and throw them at me, and fire will come out of the stones
> (and) burn you up.'

This saying is Thomas's version of the central question Jesus
puts to his disciples in Mark 8.27, 'Who do people say that I
am?' Thomas's answer receives praise from Jesus, who has
successfully transmitted knowledge to the best student. Jesus
is someone with whom no comparisons can be made.

Saying 114 concludes the Gospel:

> Simon Peter said to them: 'Let Mariham go out from among
> us, for women are not worthy of the life.' Jesus said: 'Look, I
> will lead her that I may make her male, in order that she too
> may become a living spirit resembling you males. For every
> woman who makes herself male will enter into the kingdom
> of heaven.'

This saying indicates a controversy between Simon Peter and
Mary Magdalene found elsewhere. It reflects a debate about
the place of women in the community: some thought women
worthy of inclusion while others disagree, proposing transformation. The saying inevitably raises the questions of what
it might mean 'to make oneself male' and with whom Jesus
sides in this debate.

Other sayings of *Thomas* may help us to interpret saying
114 in answering these questions. For example, in saying 22
Jesus discusses entering the kingdom:

> Jesus said to them: 'When you make the two into one and
> when you make the inside like the outside and the outside like
> the inside and the above like the below – that is, to make the
> male and the female into a single one, so that the male will not
> be male and the female will not be female – and when you
> make eyes instead of an eye and a hand instead of a hand
> and a foot instead of a foot, an image instead of an image,
> then you will enter [the kingdom].'

As noted, overcoming division to become a single one is a
key theme of *Thomas*. If we apply that notion to saying 114, a
woman is made male by going back to an undivided state of

Adam in the garden before the division into male and female. While some have argued that this state resembles the male more than the female in terms of the language with which it is described, it is more correctly a 'living spirit' of Genesis, namely the primal sexually undifferentiated human being. Thus although saying 114 looks anti-female, it nonetheless indicates the fluidity of gender categories. And it doesn't reinscribe Jesus' masculinity, for otherwise why would he defend Mary or how could he say to Peter, 'resembling *you* males' (emphasis added)?

text box 'Gospel beginnings' on p. 105 and then answer the following questions.

Questions

1 A good way to read the opening of Mark's Gospel actively is by reading it out loud:

> The beginning of the good news of Jesus Christ [Son of God] as it is written in Isaiah the prophet: Behold! I am sending my messenger before your face, who will organize your way; the voice of one crying in the desert, 'Prepare the way of the Lord, Make his paths straight!' John the baptizer appeared in the desert preaching a baptism of repentance for the forgiveness of sins and all the country of Judaea went out to him and all the inhabitants of Jerusalem and they were baptized by him in the Jordan river confessing their sins. Now John was clothed in the skin of camels and he wore a leather belt around his loins and was eating locusts and wild honey and he preached saying: 'There comes one stronger than I after me of whom I am not worthy, stooping down to loosen the strap of his sandals. I baptize you with water but he will baptize you with holy spirit'; and it happened in those days Jesus came from Nazareth of Galilee and was baptized in the Jordan by John and immediately, coming up out of the water he saw the heavens split open and the spirit coming down as a dove on him and a voice came from the heavens: 'You are my son the beloved, in you I am well-pleased', and the spirit drove him into the desert and he was in the desert forty days being tempted by Satan and

he was with the wild beasts and the angels served him. Now after the arrest of John, Jesus came into Galilee preaching the gospel of God and saying, 'The time is fulfilled and the kingdom of God has come near; repent and believe in the gospel.' (Mark 1.1–15)

(a) What do you notice after hearing these opening verses?
(b) What is being conveyed here?
(c) Compare the opening of Matthew's Gospel (Matthew 1.1–17) to the opening of Mark. What differing impressions does the reader get from these two openings?

2 Compare the following two translations of Matthew 1.2:

KJV: Abraham begat Isaac; and Isaac begat Jacob; and Jacob begat Judas and his brethren;
NRSV: Abraham was the father of Isaac, and Isaac the father of Jacob, and Jacob the father of Judah and his brothers,

(a) What are the differences between these two translations?
(b) What is the function of the genealogy in Matthew?
(c) What are the consequences of the absence of a genealogy from Mark's Gospel?
(d) Why does Matthew include women in the genealogy? Who are they?

3 Read Matthew's account of who Jesus was and whence he came in Matthew 1—2. Notice the repeated use of the formula, 'this took place so as to fulfil the words of the prophet X' followed by a particular citation.

(a) Which parts of Scripture is Matthew using?
(b) What is Matthew's attitude to these Scriptures?

4 Compare the following texts from Luke and Josephus' *Against Apion*:

Luke 1.1–4: Since many have undertaken to set down an orderly account of the events that have been fulfilled among us, just as they were handed on to us by those who from the beginning were eyewitnesses and servants of the word, I too decided, after investigating everything carefully from the very first, to write an orderly account for you, most excellent Theophilus, so that you may know the truth concerning the things about which you have been instructed.

Against Apion 1: Through my treatise on Ancient History, most eminent Epaphroditus, I consider that, to those who will read it, I have made it sufficiently clear concerning our people, the Judaeans, that it is extremely ancient and had its own original composition, and how it inhabited the land that we now possess; for I composed in the Greek language a history covering 5,000 years, on the basis of our sacred books.

However, since I see that a considerable number of people pay attention to the slanders spread by some out of malice, and disbelieve what I have written on ancient history, but adduce as proof that our people is of more recent origin that it was not thought worthy of any mention by the most renowned Greek historians, I thought it necessary to write briefly on all these matters, to convict those who insult us as guilty of malice and deliberate falsehood, to correct the ignorance of others, and to instruct all who wish to know the truth on the subject of our antiquity.

(a) What do Luke's and Josephus' openings have in common?
(b) What is the style and purpose of Luke's preface? (It is also helpful to read Acts 1 as the introduction to the second part of a two-volume work.)
(c) What is the author's relationship to eyewitness reports?
(d) If Theophilus is a Gentile and an interested patron for whom Luke writes, in what ways might the narrative of Luke–Acts demonstrate his interests and concerns?

2. Accounts of Jesus' baptism

The accounts of Jesus' baptism differ among the Gospels. Only Mark and Matthew agree that John baptized Jesus. In Luke, John is not identified as the agent of baptism (he is removed from the scene) and in John's Gospel, the baptism is not recorded. It is possible to see the different emphases of the Gospel writers in their various accounts of Jesus' baptism (see Table 3 overleaf).

Questions

1 Read Mark 1. What is the purpose of the baptism in Mark's Gospel? Why was Jesus baptized?

Table 3: Accounts of Jesus' baptism

Mark 1.9–11	Matthew 3.13–17	Luke 3.19	
		But Herod the ruler, who had been rebuked by him because of Herodias, his brother's wife, and because of all the evil things that Herod had done, added to them all by shutting up John in prison.	
In those days Jesus came from Nazareth of Galilee and was baptized by John in the Jordan.	Then Jesus came from Galilee to John at the Jordan, to be baptized by him. John would have prevented him, saying, 'I need to be baptized by you, and do you come to me?' But Jesus answered him, 'Let it be so now; for it is proper for us in this way to fulfil all righteousness.' Then he consented.	*Luke 3.21–22*	*John 1.32–34* And John testified, 'I saw the Spirit descending from heaven like a dove, and it remained on him. I myself did not know him, but the one who sent me to baptize with water said to me, "He on whom you see the Spirit descend and remain is the one who baptizes with the Holy Spirit."
And just as he was coming up out of the water, he saw the heavens torn apart and the Spirit descending like a dove on him. And a voice came from heaven, 'You are my Son, the Beloved; with you I am well pleased.'	And when Jesus had been baptized, just as he came up from the water, suddenly the heavens were opened to him and he saw the Spirit of God descending like a dove and alighting on him. And a voice from heaven said, 'This is my Son, the Beloved, with whom I am well pleased.'	Now when all the people were baptized, and when Jesus also had been baptized and was praying, the heaven was opened, and the Holy Spirit descended upon him in bodily form like a dove. And a voice came from heaven, 'You are my Son, the Beloved; with you I am well pleased.'	And I myself have seen and have testified that this is the Son of God.'

2 Why does Matthew's account of Jesus' baptism include a dialog between Jesus and John the Baptist? What does it say about the relationship between John and Jesus?

3 If John's Gospel has no account of Jesus' baptism, why does the Gospel include John the Baptist (John 1.6–35; 3.27–30; 5.33–36)?

3. Radical discipleship and household division

Following Jesus into a community of disciples who preach of God's dynamic realm nevertheless brings about household conflict. In Luke 12.51–53 Jesus says:

> Do you think that I have come to bring peace to the earth? No, I tell you, but rather division! From now on five in one household will be divided, three against two and two against three;
>   they will be divided:
>   father against son
>   and son against father,
>   mother against daughter
>   and daughter against mother,
>   mother-in-law against her daughter-in-law
>   and daughter-in-law against mother-in-law.

Matthew adds to this Q saying, 'and one's foes will be members of one's own household' (Matthew 10.34–36).

Questions

1 How many people live in this household? (The passage assumes the presence of slaves.)

2 Where does division occur?

3 Which generation follows Jesus out of the household? Who is left in a household once family members have left to follow Jesus?

4 What does this say about Jesus' pragmatic choice of followers? (Read Luke 5.1–11 where Jesus calls Simon with James and John, partners in a fishing guild and brothers.)

Table 4: The parable of the sower

Saying 9 of the Gospel of Thomas	*Mark 4.3–9*	*Luke 8.5–8*
Jesus said, 'Look, the Sower went out, took a handful (of seeds) and scattered (them). Some fell on the road, and the birds came and pecked them up. Others fell on rock, did not take root in the soil, and did not produce heads of grain. Others fell on thorns; they choked the seeds and worms ate them. And others fell on good soil, and it produced a good crop: it bore sixty per measure and one hundred and twenty per measure.'	'Listen! A sower went out to sow. And as he sowed, some seed fell on the path, and the birds came and ate it up. Other seed fell on rocky ground, where it did not have much soil, and it sprang up quickly, since it had no depth of soil. And when the sun rose, it was scorched; and since it had no root, it withered away. Other seed fell among thorns, and the thorns grew up and choked it, and it yielded no grain. Other seed fell into good soil and brought forth grain, growing up and increasing and yielding thirty and sixty and a hundredfold.' And he said, 'Let anyone with ears to hear listen!'	'A sower went out to sow his seed; and as he sowed, some fell on the path and was trampled on, and the birds of the air ate it up. Some fell on the rock; and as it grew up, it withered for lack of moisture. Some fell among thorns, and the thorns grew with it and choked it. Some fell into good soil, and when it grew, it produced a hundredfold.' As he said this, he called out, 'Let anyone with ears to hear listen!'
	Mark 4.10–12	*Luke 8.9–11*
	When he was alone, those who were around him along with the twelve asked him about the parables. And he said to them, 'To you has been given the secret of the kingdom of God, but for those outside, everything comes in parables; in order that "they may indeed look, but not perceive, and may indeed listen, but not understand; so that they may not turn again and be forgiven".'	Then his disciples asked him what this parable meant. He said, 'To you it has been given to know the secrets of the kingdom of God; but to others I speak in parables, so that "looking they may not perceive, and listening they may not understand". Now the parable is this: The seed is the word of God.'

4. The *Gospel of Thomas*

The *Gospel of Thomas* has caused controversy in the scholarly community, with some scholars arguing that it is an independent witness to sayings of Jesus also found in the Synoptic Gospels. In this regard, parts of the text could be dated to the first century. Other scholars argue that it postdates the New Testament Gospels and think it shows at least a tendency towards Gnosticism. Read the text box on 'Gnosticism and the *Gospel of Thomas*' on p. 119 and then answer the following questions.

Questions

1 Compare the parable of the Sower in *Thomas*, Mark and Luke (see Table 4). What similarities and differences do you notice? How would you explain them?

2 Which sayings in the *Gospel of Thomas* seem most unlike the sayings in the canonical Gospels? (Compare, for example, saying 107 with Luke 15.3–7, and saying 19 with Mark 8.14–21.) How would these affect one's image of Jesus?

3 Find out about Gnosticism and the *Gospel of Thomas* by reading Meyer and Valantasis, and then answer the following questions:

  (a) What elements in the *Gospel of Thomas* seem most 'Gnostic'?
  (b) Do we find evidence of any of these elements in New Testament writings? How does one determine what qualifies as a 'Gnostic' saying? Might a Gnostic source include sayings that are not Gnostic?

Further reading

Stephen C. Barton (ed.), *The Cambridge Companion to the Gospels* (Cambridge: Cambridge University Press, 2006)

Richard Burridge, *What are the Gospels? A Comparison with Greco-Roman Biography* (Cambridge: Cambridge University Press, 1992)

Mark Goodacre, *The Case Against Q: Studies in Markan Priority and the Synoptic Problem* (Harrisburg, Pennsylvania: Trinity Press International, 2002)

Karen H. Jobes and Moisés Silva, *Invitation to the Septuagint* (Grand Rapids, Michigan: Baker Academic, 2005)

Helmut Koester and James M. Robinson, *Trajectories through Early Christianity* (Philadelphia: Fortress, 1971)

Marvin Meyer, *The Gospel of Thomas: The Hidden Sayings of Jesus* (San Francisco: HarperCollins, 1992)

Albert Pietersma and Benjamin G. Wright, *A New English Translation of the Septuagint* (New York: Oxford University Press, 2007)

Richard Valantasis, *The Gospel of Thomas*, New Testament Readings (London: Routledge, 1997)

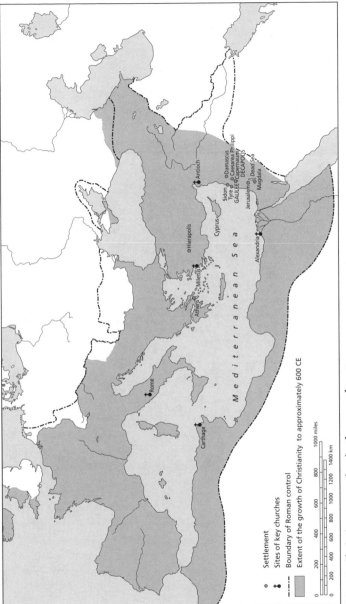

Settlement

Sites of key churches

Boundary of Roman control

Extent of the growth of Christianity to approximately 600 CE

Map 3 Christian expansion in the second century

Figure 4. Pergamon altar frieze: King Eumenes II built an altar to Zeus on Pergamon's acropolis during the second century B.C.E.. The altar and frieze, today in Berlin's Pergamon Museum, celebrates the achievements of the royal family and epitomizes Hellenistic sculpture. It is widely thought to be the reference of Satan's "throne" in Revelation 2:13. *Photo courtesy of Wikimedia Commons (public domain inage).*

4

Catholic and apocalyptic writings

The New Testament is available today as a collection of writings that the Church consults as the word of God. Many readers think of the New Testament when they read the statement attributed to Paul (2 Timothy 3.16), 'All Scripture is God-inspired and useful for teaching, for reproof, for correction, and for training in righteousness.' But at the time of the Pastoral Epistles (1 and 2 Timothy and Titus) a generation after Paul's death, the 'Scripture' concerned was the Bible of Israel, available to most Christian congregations in the Greek translation known as the Septuagint.

Some additional material appears in the Greek Bible, including wholly new books such as Tobit and supplements to books in Hebrew, which do not appear in the Hebrew Bible. These additions are known as the Apocrypha (because it was once thought their Hebrew originals were 'hidden', which is what the word *apokrupha* means in Greek, although in many cases the texts were actually composed in Greek). Gradually, however, the letters of Paul, the Synoptic Gospels, and writings attributed to Paul after his death became a part of worship in the Church alongside Israel's Scriptures in their fuller, Greek form, with the Apocrypha. The existence of the Apocrypha, effectively an expanded Greek version of Israel's Scriptures, helped prepare the way for the emergence of the Greek New Testament.

The second-century teacher Justin Martyr referred to the Gospels today included in the New Testament as 'memoirs of the apostles' (*Apology* 66.3). By his time, a powerful new concept had become current among the followers of Jesus: they believed that God directly addressed the Church *at large*, not only individual congregations, by means of what the apostles said in their writings, and that the apostolic message concerned the ultimate fate of all humanity and the end of the world as we know it.

Box 4.1. Justin Martyr

Justin Martyr (100–165) is one of the earliest defenders of the Christian faith. He wrote his *Apology* in 151 c.e. in order to prove the injustice of the persecution of the Christians. In *Apology* 66 he writes:

> For the apostles, in the memoirs composed by them, which are called Gospels, have thus delivered unto us what was enjoined upon them; that Jesus took bread, and when He had given thanks, said, 'This do in remembrance of Me, this is My body;' and that, after the same manner, having taken the cup and given thanks, He said, 'This is My blood;' and gave it to them alone.

This conviction insisted that the words of the apostles were universal, or 'catholic' (*katholikos*) in the language of the time, and that they included apocalyptic truth. The word 'apocalyptic' comes from the Greek word *apokalupsis*, which means 'uncovering', 'disclosure' or 'revelation'. Scholars speak of 'apocalyptic' in reference to a type of literature produced by religious communities that deny the reality of this world and look forward to its supersession by a future, divinely ordered world. As a literary style, apocalyptic claims to be a revelation by God of his purpose for his chosen people and for the future of the creation. It uses visions, oracles, symbols, and cryptic language to convey its message, since the import of such writing is intended only for the inner group, the guardians of the worldview of the community involved. The community of God's people is typically called upon to accept suffering and even martyrdom during the present period of cosmic struggle, but they are given assurance that they will be vindicated and will enjoy new life in the age to come.

Since the Enlightenment scholars have often downplayed the apocalyptic aspect of the New Testament, because it contradicts the picture of a stable, static universe that became fashionable during the eighteenth century. Yet belief in a finite world whose end (*eskhaton* in Greek) was to come soon was common to ancient thought, emerging in Christianity, Judaism and Stoicism, for example.

The eschatological expectations of Christianity varied, but a commitment to eschatology, and to the conviction that the apostolic message addressed the Church as a whole, not merely particular localities, remain facts that need explanation.

The dating of the individual documents that voice this consensus is still open to discussion, and several of them found their way among the books accepted in the New Testament only late and with difficulty. Seven of them (the Letter of James, 1 Peter, 2 Peter, 1 John, 2 John, 3 John and Jude) are known as the Catholic Epistles, since they address Christians beyond particular communities. After they have been considered, we will complete our discussion of books of the New Testament by turning to other works produced after the destruction of the Temple in 70 c.e. (Mark 13; Matthew 24—25; Luke 21; 2 Thessalonians; Acts; and the Revelation to John) that show how a catholic consensus emerged out of apocalyptic convictions.

The Catholic Epistles

While it is convenient to consider these writings in their order of appearance in the Bible, no conclusions can be drawn from that order in regard to the date of any individual work.

James

The Epistle of James owes its appearance here, as the first document after the 14 letters attributed to Paul, to its claim that James, the brother of Jesus, was the author. That stance permits this Epistle to set out an understanding of the Christian faith that differs clearly and deliberately from Paul's. 'Show me your faith without works, and I will show you faith by my works' (James 2.18b, c) – this challenge seems a precise response to a version of Paul's teaching (see, for example, Romans 3.19–20). But although a debate with several of Paul's themes and expressions shines through the Epistle of James, its main concern is not to confuse active faith with theology: 'Pure and blameless religion before God and Father is this: to visit orphans and widows in their tribulation and to keep oneself spotless from the world' (James 1.27).

Wealth is the particular temptation that the Epistle of James identifies on several occasions (1.10–11; 2.1–7; 5.1–6), as a perversion within the community and a cause for the apocalyptic judgment of God. Pressing his case home, the author not only challenges the teaching of Paul, but also invokes the authority of *1 Enoch* (in 5.1). This work is not a part of the Hebrew Bible, and it does not feature in the Apocrypha. But it was a widely respected book in Jewish antiquity, belonging to what it is known today as the 'Pseudepigrapha'. That term is used to refer to 'falsely attributed writing'; in this case, it is obvious that the antediluvian Enoch did not actually write *1 Enoch*. In antiquity, however, the wisdom of Enoch was revered, and portions of his alleged book were discovered among the Dead Sea Scrolls.

Unlike others of the Catholic Epistles, James sees wealth rather than persecution as the principal obstacle to faith, although the fact of bearing reproach for proclaiming the name of Christ is acknow-

---

Box 4.2. Pseudepigrapha and Apocrypha

The authors of the Catholic Epistles and apocalyptic writings in the New Testament were aware of works which are now described as part of the 'Old Testament Pseudepigrapha'. The term 'Pseudepigrapha' means 'falsely titled'. It describes writings falsely attributed to figures mentioned in the Hebrew Bible such as Enoch. The term is used today as a means to classify not describe these writings. Pseudepigrapha mostly date from 200 B.C.E. to 200 C.E. and include *1, 2* and *3 Enoch*, *2 Baruch*, *4 Ezra* and the *Testaments of the Twelve Patriarchs*. Ideas in the Pseudepigrapha help to explain features of the New Testament.

The term 'Apocrypha' (Greek: hidden) generally refers to Jewish writings dating from 300 B.C.E. to 70 C.E. incorporated into the Roman Catholic and Orthodox Old Testaments. They include: Tobit, Judith, additions to the book of Esther, Wisdom of Solomon, Sirach, Baruch, Epistle of Jeremiah, Prayer of Azariah and the Song of the Three Jews, Susannah, Bel and the Dragon, 1 and 2 Maccabees, 1 Esdras, the Prayer of Manassah and 2 Esdras. Quite often these books were deemed appropriate, not for public worship, but for private devotional usage.

ledged (2.7). Taking these indications together, along with the earliest knowledge of this Epistle in the East rather than the West, recent scholarship has suggested that James originated in Syria, and offers an alternative vision to the emerging hierarchy of the Church elsewhere in the Roman empire.

Instead of using the language of a 'manager' or 'bishop' (*episkopos*) as the leader of a given community, James refers to the authority of carefully chosen 'teachers' (3.1–2) and 'elders' (5.14), the former concerned with wisdom as a gift bestowed by 'the Father of lights' (1.16–18) and the latter with prayer. James also sees the community as a 'synagogue' (2.2), and calls his readers 'the twelve tribes in the Diaspora' (1.1). The author is remarkably different from the historical James, in making no mention of the Temple or laws of purity, and it has been recognized since antiquity that the work is pseudonymous (see Jerome, writing in 393; *De viris illustribus* 2.2). But the author nonetheless sponsors a kind of Christianity, loyal to what he calls 'the law of liberty' (1.25; 2.12) that stands in the line of the historical James' dedication to the Torah. In common with the Gospel according to Matthew, with which it shares a good deal of material, the Epistle of James uses the Greek term *parousia* to speak of the coming of Christ in final judgment (James 5.7–8), and this is an indication of both its Syrian origin and its relatively late date, probably during the last decade of the first century.

1 Peter

During the same period of time, another pseudonymous work, called the First Letter of Peter, was directed to a circle of churches in Asia Minor. In several ways, 1 Peter is comparable to the Epistle of James: in both letters, for example, temptations or tests (*peirasmoi* in Greek) are to be welcomed as proving one's worth (1 Peter 1.6–7; James 1.2–4), and the 'word' of God has power to redeem believers (1 Peter 1.23; James 1.21). The social settings of these two Epistles, however, are quite different. While wealth besets the readers of James, the issue that concerns 1 Peter throughout is the ambient oppression of believers; this letter openly and proudly uses the term 'Christian', a term coined by outsiders (4.16), in order to refer to the marginalization of believing communities. Believers occupy servant classes in a series of passages that call readers to blameless conduct, even in the face of oppression (1 Peter 2.11–25; 3.8–17; 4.12–19). Like James, but more insistently, 1 Peter refers to the impending judgment of God through Christ as a principal motivation, preferring the term 'apocalypse' (1 Peter 1.7, 13) to 'parousia', and specifying that it brings the end of all time (*eskhaton ton khronon*, 1.20), or the 'finish of all things' (4.7), a fiery judgment (4.12–19) whose prelude is the current oppression by the devil (5.8–9).

The First Epistle of Peter acknowledges the estrangement of his readers from their social environment, also using the term 'Diaspora' (1.1), as in the opening of James, and calling them 'homeless and sojourners' (2.11). The term for 'homeless', *paroikos* in Greek, came to be used of a 'parish', the scope of a Christian community. In 1 Peter, the homeless, those who recognize that their home is not to be found in the world of convention, are invited to be incorporated as 'living stones' into Christ, who is the first living stone or 'rock' (a play on the name for Peter; 1 Peter 2.4–10). With an ease that characterizes the Catholic Epistles as a whole, 1 Peter embraces a theology like that of the Epistle to the Hebrews, where a heavenly temple replaces the edifice lost on the earth, much as it echoes Paul's teaching in regard to baptism (1 Peter 3.18—4.6), in which every believer dies with Christ in order to be raised with him from enslaving sin (Romans 6.3–11). With deft understatement, and occasional and carefully contained poetry, 1 Peter sets out how those who hear the call of Christ are included within a new temple that is the first stage in the transformation of the entire world.

Although the author, writing as Peter, refers to himself as an 'elder' (*presbuteros*, the term that entered English as 'priest'; 1 Peter 5.1), the first title he uses is 'apostle' (1.1). In this, he accords more with the Pauline writings than with James. Similarly, the term for 'manager' or 'bishop' (*episkopos*; 2.25) is applied to Christ himself, and is also used in a verbal form for how the 'elders' are to 'manage' their flocks (5.2). This brings the language of leadership into the social vocabulary of 1 Peter's audience. Even a servant might be tasked with management; in fact, mismanagement is one of the accusations that Christian servants are to guard against (1 Peter 4.15). For all its appeal to the power of apocalypse to come and the spiritual temple to which believers belong, 1 Peter remains a document that addresses believers in the social circumstances of subservience and occasional oppression.

2 Peter

Among the latest works in the New Testament, if not the last, 2 Peter rides on the wings of 1 Peter by declaring itself the second Epistle of the apostle (2 Peter 3.1), although the author seems neither to be Peter nor the author of 1 Peter, but a writer with his own character. In a creative, influential phrase, 2 Peter speaks of believers becoming 'participants of divine nature' (1.4), and articulates a remarkable ladder of perfection, in which 'you produce by your faith virtue, by virtue knowledge, by knowledge temperance, by temperance endurance, by endurance piety, by piety fraternal feeling, and by fraternal feeling love' (2 Peter 1.5b–7). 'Peter' takes up the position of reminding his readers of what he has already taught (1.12–15), so that he might be remembered after his departure by this testamentary teaching.

The author contrasts apostolic authority (including his own) to the elaborate myths of competitors by referring to becoming with his apostolic colleagues 'eyewitnesses of the power and presence of our Lord Christ Jesus' (2 Peter 1.16), an apparent reference to the scene of Jesus' transfiguration before Peter, James and John in the Synoptic Gospels (see Mark 9.2–10 for the earliest version). The term for 'presence' in 2 Peter 1.16 in Greek is *parousia*, the same word used in 1 Peter for Jesus' second coming. For 2 Peter, world transformation is already happening, and is not only a promise for the future. Just as the author's sense of eschatology has shifted into the language of a ladder of discipline that leads one into the eternal, divine nature, so he also makes the claim that believers share a witness to eternal truth that is even firmer than the transfiguration. 'The prophetic word' (2 Peter 1.19), which guides all believers until the end of time, is the surest source of truth, more powerful and reliable than apostolic witness itself.

The interpretation of prophetic Scripture is the crucial issue for 2 Peter, and the bulk of the letter is taken up by arguing that purely personal readings should be subjugated to the impulse of God's Spirit (2 Peter 1.20–21). A series of texts from the Scriptures of Israel aggregate into a warning of how God punished the unrighteous from the time of Noah. These texts are conventional, and much the same material is repeated in the Epistle of Jude. In 2 Peter, however, the list of warnings is intended to demonstrate that 'If those who have fled from the pollutions of the world by the recognition of our Lord and Savior Christ Jesus, but again are involved and give way, their endings are worse than their beginnings' (2 Peter 2.20). In particular, 2 Peter targets the issue of eschatology, insisting that there is a single message through the prophets and apostles. The author quotes mockers who ask about Christ, 'Where is the promise of his *parousia*?' (2 Peter 3.4).

With his assurance that eternity and the promise of joining oneself to God's nature puts all temporal concerns into a secondary position, the author alludes to Psalm 90.4, 'This one thing should not escape you, beloved, that one day for the Lord is as a thousand years, and a thousand years as a day' (3.8). This long view of human experience, which is more properly speaking a transcendent view, takes up a theme from Paul's letters (see, for example, 1 Thessalonians 5.1–3 and 1 Corinthians 15.20–28) that the author of 2 Peter appropriates, although he cannot quite resist saying that Paul wrote some difficult passages whose meaning can be twisted by opportunists (2 Peter 3.16). The confidence of this Catholic Epistle, in taking up Paul's methods in order to correct Paul, is as stunning as its insistence that it conveys the message of Peter.

1 John

The First Epistle of John is written with a style and content comparable to the Gospel of John, including reference to the 'word of life' (1 John 1.1) and an alternation between a self-reference by the author as 'we' and 'I'. A tight relationship between the Epistle and the Gospel is evident, and – on an assumption of chronological progression within the New Testament in its present order – it has been conventional to think of 1 John as coming after the Gospel. But several themes that are carefully worked out in the Gospel (such as the 'Word' and the 'light' of the prologue), seem less developed in 1 John (chapter 1), and there are times when 1 John seems closer to imagery in the Revelation to John, for example in its emphasis on how Jesus' blood cleanses the believer from sin (1 John 1.7; 2.2; Revelation 1.5; 7.14).

Whatever the order between 1 John and the Gospel, the Epistle's emphasis on knowing God and Jesus is palpable. The issue is not only knowledge itself, but also knowing *that* one has known God, as an assurance of salvation (1 John 2.3). An ethical commitment to the commandments is said to bring that assurance (3.19–24). The crucial and at first sight abstract statement that 'God is love' (4.7–8) proceeds from this combination of ideas: the activity of loving is proof of one's rootedness in love itself, so that divine 'seed' (*sperma* 3.9) animates all that one does.

The conception of 1 John may appear comfortably Hellenistic, but its conviction that human life is in its 'last hour' is no less vigorous (1 John 2.18) than in other writings in the New Testament. The Epistle interprets false teaching as the influence of 'antichrists' in the final times. The author attributes a denial of Christ to these teachers (2.22), without much specification of what they deny, although the fact of Jesus coming 'in flesh' has clearly emerged as a crucial issue (1 John 4.2–3). The role of the devil as the source of sin (3.8) is prominent, but so is the sacramental force of baptism, Eucharist (5.6) and anointing (2.20, 27) as sources of authority that overcome all resistance.

2 and 3 John

Both the Second and the Third Epistles of John, extremely brief communications, take their stand on the basis of 1 John, the Gospel according to John, and the Revelation. These Johannine letters refer to their author as 'the elder' (*presbuteros*; 2 John 1; 3 John 1), and that suggests that an elder named Yohannan in Aramaic was their initial source. Whether the elder John should be identified as the author of the Gospel according to John, and what relationship he had to the writer of the Revelation to John, remain matters of dispute.

In both 2 John and 3 John, the author simply identifies himself as 'the elder' in order to address issues that emerged as a consequence of the Johannine literature as a whole. 2 John is especially concerned to counteract the teaching that Jesus did not come 'in flesh' (2 John 7), while 3 John is concerned either to disapprove (9–10) or approve (12) teachers who are named, but are no longer known to history, on the basis of their hospitality, which is taken to be a proof of keeping the commandment of love.

Jude

Coming as it does after 2 Peter in the New Testament, Jude can appear repetitious, since its core – examples taken from the Scriptures of Israel in order to warn Christians in the present – virtually doubles what can be read in 2 Peter, although it might be that Jude is earlier than 2 Peter. But in three ways, the originality of Jude is evident, whether or not it was composed before 2 Peter. First, this message is alleged to come from Judas, the brother of James (Jude 1), and therefore the brother of Jesus (see Mark 6.3). The fact that Jude's relationship to James (rather than Jesus) is emphasized reflects the high regard for James within Catholic Christianity as Jesus' successor. The same communication that was claimed by one part of the Church for Peter is therefore attributed to the circle of James.

Box 4.3. The *Ascension of Moses* and the Epistle of Jude

The author of the Epistle of Jude alludes to the story of the dispute between Michael and Satan over the body of Moses:

> But when the archangel Michael contended with the devil and disputed about the body of Moses, he did not dare to bring a condemnation of slander against him, but said, 'The Lord rebuke you!' (Jude 9)

This story is found in the *Ascension of Moses*, also known as the *Assumption* or *Testament of Moses*, a work of the Pseudepigrapha which describes the last words of Moses to Joshua on the basis of Deuteronomy 31–34. In it Joshua is told to record and hide prophecies concerning the nation until the appointed time. The story about the fight over Moses' body seems to have occurred in the lost ending of the *Assumption of Moses*, but can be reconstructed with some confidence.

Some scholars propose to date the text to the first century C.E. while others have argued for a date during the early stages of the Maccabean revolt in the second century B.C.E., allowing for interpolations and re-editing in the Herodian period (first century B.C.E.). The text, originally written in Hebrew, is incomplete and often illegible.

Second, as compared to 2 Peter, Jude widens its definition of the Scriptures of Israel, to include writings not included in the Hebrew Bible – notably the *Ascension of Moses* and *1 Enoch*. (During the second century, the Church reversed this inclination to widen the definition of Scripture.) Finally, Jude does not argue for the ladder of perfection developed in 2 Peter, but instead invokes the conception of a single 'faith once delivered to the saints' (Jude 3), a phrase that refers to a single substance of belief among all the patriarchs and prophets until the time of the Church.

Apocalyptic convictions

The Catholic Epistles demonstrate a combination of settled confidence and profound disagreement in regard to the end of time. They simply assume that a shift has occurred from the promises given Israel to their realization within the Church, as if this transition were self-evident. In Chapter 2, we saw that the Epistle to the Hebrews (*c*.95 C.E.) spelled out this transition in intellectual terms; that writing marked the front of the curve of Christianity's embrace of a Platonic explanation of its faith. In the way of intellectual efforts, however, Hebrews was more important for indicating what was to come on the basis of a change that had already been made than in actually making that change.

One of the great, unresolved questions in the study of the New Testament centers on the confidence of the Catholic Epistles and Hebrews in regard to both the end of the world and the independence of Christianity from Judaism. In order to understand both those developments, we need to consider writings that took the Judaic genre of apocalypse in a radically new direction.

Later Prophetic writings, such as Ezekiel and Zechariah, clearly indicate that the prophets' threat and promise of final, eschatological judgment had already made the transition to the assurance that the ultimate aim of God was already a reality in heaven, and could be related to the calendar of the earth's time. But these two aspects of apocalypse, the conviction that God's will is already accomplished even when not realized on earth, and the expectation that his will can be experienced temporally in events on earth, comes to classic expression in the book of Daniel.

Daniel was composed during the second century B.C.E., when the Seleucid monarch, Antiochus IV Epiphanes, ordered that the gods of Hellenism should be worshipped in the Temple in Jerusalem, dir-ectly threatening the scriptural guarantee that this was the site for the recognition of the one God of Israel. In response, the book of Daniel, in the name of a seer from the Babylonian period several centuries earlier, delivers its vision of a heavenly reality greater than the power of the Seleucids, which would bring about the definitive victory of Israel at a predicted point in time. The Maccabean movement in fact defeated Antiochus IV, led by a Jewish militant named Judas Maccabeus (meaning 'the hammer'), and motivated to a large extent by works such as the book of Daniel. The resulting victory was stunning but not definitive, and in the end the descendants of Judas Maccabeus could not resist Roman hegemony. Yet apocalyptic vision lived on, and emerged with fresh force whenever the Temple in Jerusalem was threatened.

The Roman siege of Jerusalem, which culminated in their burning of the Temple in 70 C.E., represented such a threat. Judaic apocalypses produced near 100 C.E., such as *4 Ezra* and *2 Baruch*, replied to this challenge. Within the movement of Jesus, the loss of the Temple was no less brutal, since it had represented the focus of major teachers, including Jesus himself, Peter, James the brother of Jesus, and Paul. As a result, a series of works were produced for Christian instruction, either in the genre of apocalypse or engaged with apocalyptic issues. Their emergence during the last quarter of the first century explains how, by the time of the Catholic Epistles, a settled eschatological confidence characterized Christian belief.

The first apocalypse written in Jesus' name appears in Mark 13, Matthew 24—25, and Luke 21. Unlike his other teaching in the Synoptic Gospels, this 'Little Apocalypse' (as it is called) is arranged as a continuous discourse, a carefully crafted speech. It comes complete with notes to the reader, in the form of a reference to the book of Daniel; the 'abomination of desolation' in the Little Apocalypse alludes to the destruction of the Temple (Mark 13.14; Matthew 24.15; Luke 21.20; cf. Daniel 11.31; 12.11). The literary structure of the discourse is so unlike the usual form of Jesus' teaching, it is generally regarded as a speech synthesized from elements of Jesus' sayings together with references to Daniel. Unlike the book

Box 4.4. *4 Ezra* and *2 Baruch*

4 Ezra purports to have been written thirty years after the destruction of Jerusalem by Babylon (556 B.C.E.), but the actual focus is several years after the Roman destruction of Jerusalem in 70 C.E., around 100 C.E.. By conflating these events from differ-ent centuries, *4 Ezra* predicts that what happened to Babylon will happen to Rome, and that just as the destruction of the First Temple was followed by a restoration, so destruction of the Second Temple will be followed by renewal. The earliest complete manuscripts are in Syriac (sixth century) and in Latin (ninth century), while the original text may have been written in Greek.

4 Ezra includes seven visions. The seer Ezra is troubled by the destruction of Jerusalem and its Temple and expresses his despair to God. The events of 70 C.E. call into question the justice of God towards his chosen people. How is God to be faithful to the everlasting covenant sworn to Abraham, if the city is destroyed? Yes, the people have broken the command-ments, but they are punished while pagan nations like Babylon and Rome prosper. For God to allow Israel to be humiliated at the hand of Babylon/Rome induces a crisis of faith resulting in an investigation of how God works in the world. An angel reassures Ezra that God loves Israel and is in control of events. Mortals, however, cannot comprehend heavenly realities. While the present time is dominated by evil, in a future age God will reward the righteous and punish the wicked. A final vision recreates Sinai, and Ezra affirms the covenant commitment of God while exhorting the people to follow the Law.

2 Baruch, like *4 Ezra*, is a response to the destruction of the Temple at the hands of the Romans that uses the con-ceit of the destruction of the First Temple by Babylon. Baruch the scribe purportedly writes the text. God had allowed the destruction of the Temple to chasten the people for their diso-bedience. But this chastening is temporary: a brighter future awaits them. God has in fact ordained the fate of the world from creation. A Messiah (Anointed One) is coming whose presence will mark the end of a period of corruption. There will be judgment for all. Those who had been faithful to the Torah would reap their reward in the Heavenly Jerusalem, an incorruptible place. The nations that had vilified God's elect will be duly punished. The story is about how a people of faith moved from intense grief to consolation, in the knowledge that an omnipotent God will always vindicate the righteous.

of Daniel, however, the Little Apocalypse steps back from calculating a calendar of the end time. It seems to move confidently in that direction, with its account of disaster and war, and the coming of the Son of Man. But then comes the warning, 'But concerning that day and hour no one knows, neither the angels in heaven nor the son, except the Father' (Mark 13.32; cf. Matthew 24.36; Acts 1.7). The association of the destruction of the Temple with the eschatological judgment, and a call to be ready for a judgment that comes as a thief in the night (1 Thessalonians 5.2; Matthew 24.43; Luke 12.39; 2 Peter 3.3; Revelation 3.10; 16.15) could confidently be presented under Jesus' name, but the New Testament presents no consistent scheme of an apocalyptic calendar, and documents that move in that direction disagree with one another when they do so.

2 Thessalonians

Much as the Little Apocalypse copes with the destruction of the Temple in Jesus' name, framing some elements from his teaching into a discourse that Jesus never actually delivered, so Paul's memory was used to develop apocalyptic teaching for a new set of circumstances in 2 Thessalonians. This work, composed around 85 C.E., refers to a necessary sequence of events prior to the end, including a desecration of the Temple (2 Thessalonians 2.3–12). Yet the purpose of referring to this sequence is not to anticipate the end, but – on the contrary – to warn against credulity: 'We ask you, brothers, concerning the *parousia* of our Lord Christ Jesus and our being gathered to him, not to be quickly shaken in mind or frightened, neither by a spirit nor a speech nor a letter as if written by us, as if the day of the Lord has come' (2 Thessalonians 2.1–2). For all the variety of the apocalyptic stances involved in the last books of the New Testament and the complex relationships among pseudonymous writings, their commonality in apocalyptic discretion is striking.

Acts

The Acts of the Apostles is composed as a companion volume to the Gospel according to Luke, and its presentation precisely explains its purpose. The risen Jesus here says to his apostles:

It is not for you to know the periods or times that the Father set by
his authority, but you shall receive power when the Holy Spirit comes
upon you and you shall be my witnesses both in Jerusalem and in
Judaea, and in Samaria and until the end of the earth. (Acts 1.7–8)

Both in what it negates and in what it asserts, this statement represents an overture to the entire program of Acts.

The power of apocalypse is here calibrated, *away* from knowing
the end and *towards* witnessing by the power of the Spirit until the
end. The first part of the statement is the equivalent of a statement
in the Little Apocalypse in the other Synoptic Gospels about the
day and hour (Mark 13.32; Matthew 24.36, cited above). The author
of Luke–Acts has acted as an editor, transplanting the warning to
its new position in order to serve as part of a deliberately framed
message. It is not the case that apocalypse disappears from the book
of Acts: to the contrary, apocalypse becomes stronger, and directs
the conduct of believers. Like the Gospel according to Luke, Acts
begins with events unfolding in the Temple within an environment
permeated by the Holy Spirit. The famous scene of Pentecost, which
fulfils the promise of Jesus, takes place in association with the Feast of
Weeks, one of the pilgrimage festivals of the Temple. Weeks occurred

---

Box 4.5. What type of book is Acts?

Scholars have differed over what 'genre' of literature Acts
is. Some have argued that it is critical history, a sequential
account of the nascent movement that became Christianity.
Others see Acts as an ancient romance in the sense of an
adventure novel describing, for example, Paul's sea travels.
This chapter explains that there are strong apocalyptic features
to the book which help to explain the perspective within which
both historical reminiscence and romantic projection have been
woven together.

Acts is generally accepted by scholars to be the second book
in a two-part work, with the Gospel of Luke being the first. Thus
if Luke and Acts are two parts of a coherent narrative then the
Lukan preface (see pp. 122–3) may introduce both works and
could influence any discussion of what kind of book Acts is.

seven weeks, or 50 days, after Passover, and is called Pentecost (from the number 50) in the Greek version of the Scriptures of Israel. Weeks or Pentecost was a pilgrimage feast that celebrated summer harvest, with produce more plentiful than at Passover, and looked ahead in the practice of Judaism to the circle of the Covenant with Moses widening to include more people by the power of the Spirit.

The stress in the narrative that the full number of the twelve (Matthias having replaced Judas; Acts 1.15–26) were together in a single place emphasizes that the gift of the Spirit pertains to Israel. Precisely at Pentecost, the Spirit is portrayed as descending on the twelve apostles, and they speak God's praises in the various languages of those assembled from the four points of the compass for that summer feast of harvest, both Jews and proselytes (Acts 2.5–12). The mention of proselytes (2.11) and the stress that those gathered came from 'every nation under heaven' (2.5) clearly point ahead to the inclusion of non-Jews by means of baptism within Acts.

The Feast of Weeks was associated with the covenant with Noah (see the non-canonical book of *Jubilees* 6.1, 10–11, 17–19, found at Qumran), the patriarch before the Israelite patriarchs, and this helps to explain why, in the minds of Peter's followers, the coming of the Spirit at Pentecost was to extend to humanity at large. Hellenistic Judaism cherished this association with Noah, because he was a paradigm of the righteous and wise non-Israelite. Even Peter's explanation of the descent of the Spirit pursues this theme (Acts 2.14–37). He quotes from the prophet Joel (2.28, in the wording of the Septuagint): 'And it will be in the last days, says God, that I will pour out from my Spirit upon all flesh.' 'All flesh', not only historic Israel, is to receive of God's Spirit; the twelve are its focus of radiation, not its limit, and Acts speaks of the baptism of some three thousand people, both Jews and converts to Judaism, in response to Peter's invitation (Acts 2.11, 41).

The structure of the book of Acts follows the program laid out in its initial statement. The opening of baptism to non-Jews occurs as a result of a vision to Peter, and his vision, like Paul's later, is detailed on three occasions. When Peter speaks in the house of the Roman centurion Cornelius in Acts 10, the Spirit falls upon the Gentiles who are listening, and those there with Peter who were circumcised are astounded 'that the gift of the Holy Spirit has been poured out even upon the nations' (10.44–45). The choice of the verb 'to pour out' is no coincidence: it is resonant with the quotation of Joel in Acts.

Indeed, those in Cornelius' house praise God 'in tongues' (10.46) in a manner reminiscent of the apostles' prophecy at Pentecost. The assumption here and in Acts 2 is that the Spirit makes people more articulate than they normally are. That is also the way Paul believes tongues are properly to be conceived, as opposed to those who see the gift of tongues as resulting in incoherence (see 1 Corinthians 14). Peter directs that this non-Jewish household be baptized 'in the name of Christ Jesus' (10.47–48). That is also the direction Peter gave earlier to his sympathetic hearers at Pentecost (2.37–38).

In the midst of great controversy concerning circumcision, Peter invokes the authority of his vision, first to the local leadership in Jerusalem (Acts 11.1–18), and then to the full apostolic meeting that concluded against requiring circumcision among believing Gentiles (Acts 15.7–11). Peter as presented in Acts comes to an expression of the Pauline school, that 'through the grace of the Lord Jesus we believe to be saved, in the manner they also shall be' (Acts 15.11, see Ephesians 2.8). Paul could scarcely have said it better himself; and that is consistent with the version of Paulinism represented in Acts.

Paul's own vision on the road to Damascus follows naturally on Peter's within the presentation of Acts, and his experience is repeated three times (Acts 9.3–9; 22.3–21; 26.9–20), just as Peter's is. In Paul's case, however, distinct changes in the presentation of the vision – changes that cannot have escaped Luke's attention – are evid-ent. In the first version, Paul's companions hear the voice speaking to Paul but see nothing (9.7), while in the second the reverse is the case (22.9); the third version does not specify the experience of Paul's companions (26.13), and in this regard it accords best of all with Paul's own reference in Galatians to a purely personal apocalypse (Galatians 1.15–16). Acts is able to convey the variety, not only of different traditions in regard to Paul, but also of how human beings can understand what is revealed to them. Visions concur with apostolic purpose, even when they differ in their details and, in the presentation of Acts, they agree with the Scriptures of Israel, and support the apostolic practice of sacraments. Within that variety, Acts discovers a unity of purpose in the extension of the message of Jesus to the ends of the earth.

That purpose includes within its reach the disclosure of God's purpose to others in the narrative of Acts, but the threefold repetition of Peter's vision as well as Paul's clearly embodies the purpose of the whole work. Paul's personal experience, not only his visions but also what happens to him in the service of the message of Jesus, is integrated within the apostolic purpose articulated by the entire work. This integration explains what might seem to be the anticlimactic ending of Acts, which puts Paul in Rome just prior to the persecution of Christians that Nero unleashed in 64 C.E., and so omits reference to those dramatic events. But that poignant moment is deliberately chosen. The choice of ending enables Acts to set out an ideal moment, prior to Paul's death and Peter's, as paradigm of what can be. In that paradigm, Paul can preach unhindered, because the Roman authorities understand he poses no threat to civic order (Acts 28.30–31).

That political dimension of Acts' closing image was obviously important to its original hearers and readers. Both Luke and Acts are addressed to a Roman official (real or, more likely, imagined) named Theophilus (Luke 1.3; Acts 1.1). Luke refers to him with the same title, 'most excellent', that Paul uses in relation to Festus (Acts 26.25): peace with Rome is a priority of this two-volume work.

Paul's last words in Acts come in the form of a citation from the book of Isaiah, which speaks of God hardening the heart of his people, so that they do not repent and he does not heal them (Acts 28.26–27; cf. Isaiah 6.9–10). This is a more extensive version of the same citation attributed to Jesus in Luke (8.10), and it is pointed against those of Israel who do not accept the message of Jesus. Luke–Acts uses this prophetic position in order to explain the Jewish rejection of Jesus' message: because the people who should have received the message did not, the opening to the Gentiles becomes inevitable. This uniquely Lukan theme appears in the Gospel (Luke 4.25–30) as well as in Acts (Acts 13.46–48), and it is Paul's final word (Acts 28.28).

The Revelation to John

The Revelation to John, written *c.*100 C.E. as an apocalypse to supplement the Gospel according to John and the Johannine Epistles, is directed as an Epistle to a circle of churches in Asia Minor that lay to the south of those addressed in 1 Peter. Yet because the Revelation was subject to considerable dispute in regard to its place in the canon, when it was finally accorded its position as the last writing in the New Testament, it was not classed among the Catholic Epistles. Instead, it has rightly been regarded as an apocalyptic work, in the line of Zechariah and Daniel and *4 Ezra*. Like those works, the Revelation presents a detailed scenario of the last times, and it builds upon the prophecies of previous writings, often citing them verbatim or alluding to their imagery.

Yet the Revelation to John is also unusual in comparison to those writings. One of the characteristics of apocalyptic discourses is that the seer assumes the identity of a prophet from previous centuries. In that way, he can take up the position of someone who predicts the future for most of human history until its very last moment, the time of the writing itself. No such claim of antiquity is involved in the Revelation to John.

The 'John' of this prophecy is not even identified. *Yochanan* in Aramaic was a very common name, shared, for example, by John the Baptist and the apostle, John the son of Zebedee. If the putative seer is John the son of Zebedee, who must have died by the end of the first century, the work is not only pseudonymous, but also assumes the perspective of a slightly earlier time. But that retrospective shift is not at all as great as in the case of other apocalypses, and in any case the *Yochanan* at issue may well be a later figure, who numbered among the disciples of Jesus but who did not number among his first apostles. However one identifies the author of the Revelation, the work does not involve the radical pseudonymity of other apocalyptic works. That is ironic, since the very terms 'apocalypse' and 'apocalyptic' are derived from the title of this, the last book of the New Testament.

Vision is the explicit genre of the entire work, and its assumption is that the world of vision is open to believers as a whole. For this reason, John dates his experience as 'on the Lord's day' (1.10), and the book's imagery develops from being involved in worship into an ever-deeper perception into heaven. The line between literal vision and heavenly vision is deliberately blurred from the outset, and it is possible that the identity of John is also a matter of conscious ambiguity. The author of the Revelation wants it understood both

Box 4.6. The canon of the New Testament and *Codex Sinaiticus*

This chapter mentions pseudepigraphic texts called the *Assumption* or *Testament of Moses* and the book of *Enoch* used by Jude. Such discussions allude to the question of books included or excluded from the New Testament and the history of the canon. The term canon (Greek: rule, measurement) denotes the 27 books comprising the New Testament. It is widely recognized that the development of the canon took place over several centuries and that by the end of the second century there was no completely fixed canon but rather collections like that of Paul's letters and of the four Gospels called 'Scripture'. Thus for New Testament writers the canon does not exist. They cited as authoritative some texts that came to be rejected, as in the cases of *1 Enoch* and the *Ascension of Moses*. By the end of the fourth century there was a consensus on the majority of the 27 books that make up the NT. One interesting piece of data in this complicated story is the development of the book, or codex. The creation of the codex in the fourth century coincided with the emergence of a fixed biblical canon. The most famous is *Codex Sinaiticus*.

Codex Sinaiticus, dated to the mid-fourth century, is the earliest complete copy of the New Testament and the predecessor of bound copies of the Bible. *Codex Sinaiticus* contains over 400 large leaves (pages) of animal skin, partly calf, on which half of the Old Testament and Apocrypha (2 Esdras, Tobit, Judith, 1 and 4 Maccabees, Wisdom and Sirach), and all of the New Testament together with the Epistle of *Barnabas* and the *Shepherd of Hermas* is written. Named after the monastery of St Catherine on Mount Sinai where it was detected by Constantine von Tischendorf in the nineteenth century, 347 leaves of the *Codex* are now in the British Library. Eleven unpublished leaves from Genesis at the beginning and the *Shepherd of Hermas* at the end of the *Codex* remain in the monastery of St Catherine, while 43 leaves are at the University Library in Leipzig and parts of five leaves are at the National Library of Russia in St Petersburg. An estimated 330 leaves, completing the Old Testament in Greek, are now lost.

The contents of codices like *Codex Sinaiticus* tell us about books the Church believed to be sacred. The fourth-century *Codex Vaticanus* contains Greek texts of the Hebrew Bible and the New Testament as well as several apocryphal books: Judith, Tobit, 2 Esdras, Baruch and the Epistle of Jeremiah.

Codex Sinaiticus is being reunited digitally for the first time since the fourth century and is now online. See <http://www.codex-sinaiticus.net/en/> for details.

that his vision has the status of prophecy, and as such should be kept in writing (1.2–3), and that this vision is accessible to all those who believe.

The Revelation initially takes the form of a letter, written to seven churches in Asia Minor at the behest of the risen Jesus (1.11). Deep divisions become apparent, as when the vision approves hating 'the Nicolaitans' (2.6, 15) and calls Jewish opponents 'the synagogue of Satan' (2.9; 3.9). These groups are not well identified as to their teaching, and the level of generality approximates to that of the Catholic Epistles. In one respect, however, the Revelation is quite clear in opposing Pauline teaching: it states that food sacrificed to idols should not be eaten (2.20–23). A prophetess in Thyatira who said that it could be (which was also the position of Paul in 1 Corinthians 6.1–6), is styled as Jezebel, accused of fornication, and threatened with the death of her children.

The link between eating food sacrificed to idols and fornication had been a dominant teaching in the Church since it was set out in a letter authorized by James, the brother of Jesus, which is quoted in the book of Acts (15.29), where James prohibits all believers, Jews and Gentiles, from eating food sacrificed to idols. The Revelation simply follows in the line of this teaching in opposition to Paul's more relaxed view of the subject. James' teaching was widespread, and its reflection within the Revelation serves to strengthen the impression that we are dealing with a general communication intended for the Church at large.

At the same time, the Revelation is a trenchantly visionary work, which presents itself as a communication of precise visions and a guide to explain how they can be understood. Although the initial 'letters' to the seven churches are so general as to be catholic, the book introduces its core with the opening of a gate or door in heaven (Revelation 4.1), which invites the seer to be shown the mysteries that surround the Throne of God in the following chapters. The divine Throne had long featured in prophetic literature before John wrote his apocalypse. Visionary narratives include those of Moses (Exodus 24.9–11), Isaiah (6.1–4), Ezekiel (1.4–28) Zechariah (3.1–9), and Daniel (7.9–14), all of which find citations or allusions in the Revelation to John. Detailed though those visions often are, in its extent and depth, the Revelation represents a conscious synthesis and extension of their imagery.

Within that synthesis, the Revelation strikes a fine balance between its apocalyptic uncovering as a vision of what already is in heaven and a prediction of what is about to happen on earth. The initial opening of heaven, for example, invites the seer, 'Come up here, and I will show you what will have to happen after these things' (4.1). What immediately follows, however, is not predictive, but a pure vision of heaven. For the remainder of the work, heaven and earth are kept in a parallax perspective, so that it is open to interpretation whether precise historical events can be specified. The success of the Revelation's parallax vision is shown in later interpretation of its complex images and numerology, which have been applied to, among other events, the French Revolution, the American Civil War, the First World War, the collapse of the Soviet Union and the conflict between Palestinians and Israelis.

It is conventional to associate interpretation of the Revelation with fundamentalist Christianity, and there is no doubt that a vehement insistence that they alone hold the keys to the correct understanding of the work is characteristic of, for example, Jehovah's Witnesses, Seventh Day Adventists and the purveyors of the books and films in the series called Left Behind. The result has been that, just as the Revelation had trouble making its way into the canon until the fourth century, so academic theology has not privileged the book during the modern period. Visions have been treated with considerable embarrassment since the Enlightenment. Yet the fact is that the Revelation is the conscious capstone of a deep strand of religious experience and of literary expression that runs through the whole of biblical literature.

Moreover, the imagery of the Revelation has proved central to currents of interpretation quite opposed to fundamentalism. During the eighteenth century, the American Quaker John Woolman made the book central in his opposition to every aspect of the institution of slavery. In 1950, Pope Pius XII declared as dogma the 'bodily Assumption of the Virgin Mary into heaven', which is currently acknowledged in Roman Catholicism as a teaching warranted by papal infallibility. One of the buttresses of Pius' argument was a vision in Revelation 12, of a woman who appeared as 'a great sign' in heaven (12.1). It is said of this woman that, having delivered a child and being attacked by a serpent, 'the two wings of a great eagle were given, so she might fly from the face of the serpent into the wilderness to her place, where she is nourished for a time and times and half a time' (Revelation 12.14). Although the imagery of the woman indeed seems to invoke the memory of Mary, the mother of Jesus, she is nowhere identified as such, and seems also to symbolize the Church in its persecution under Domitian. In this case, as in the claims of some fundamentalist groups, the attempt to limit the meaning of the Revelation falls foul of its skilful interweaving of experience on earth with visions of heaven.

In a reference back to the book of Deuteronomy (4.2), the Revelation condemns adding or subtracting from its prophecy (Revelation 22.18–19), witnessing to the integrity of its own mystery. Rather than offering precise guidance on how its text might be read as a calendar, the Revelation insists upon the resonance of its guiding apocalypses until the moment when the Lord comes again. Two of these apocalypses, developed throughout the book, are especially helpful for orienting oneself in reading the text and understanding its purpose. Both these apocalyptic images bear a palpable relationship to images in the Gospel according to John, suggesting there is a relationship between the two works. In each case, the Revelation appears closer to Judaic tradition, while the Gospel develops its more philosophical presentation. That relationship suggests that the Revelation might be closer than the Gospel to the initial teaching of the 'elder', the author of the First Letter of John, whose teaching was adapted by the editorial group that identifies itself as 'we' (rather than 'I') in the Gospel according to John. Whatever the connections among the Johannine literature,

Box 4.7. Misogyny and the Revelation to John

Feminine imagery in the Revelation is patriarchal. Women or female figures are caricatures: harlots, virgins or mothers. Rome, the city of Babylon, is described as a whore (17.4), that is idolatrous. Another woman can be described as clothed with the sun, 'with the moon under her feet' (12.1), and the new Jerusalem is portrayed as 'coming down out of heaven from God, as a bride adorned for her husband' (21.2). A woman prophet in the community at Thyatira is called 'Jezebel' by the author (2.18–29). Behind this condemnation, we may identify a real woman prophet with a following in the community. But the author removes her name and criticizes the practice of eating food sacrificed to idols, using adultery with her as a metaphor for idolatry:

> Beware, I am throwing her on a bed, and those who commit adultery with her I am throwing into great distress, unless they repent of her doings; and I will strike her children dead.
>
> (2.22–23)

By using misogynist and other imagery in the service of its anti-Rome sentiment, the Revelation reflects a symbolic world that has been uncritically read in the past as sanctioning mistreatment of women. Rejoicing over the fall of Babylon as an enactment of the fall of Rome may be cathartic as a means of celebrating God's defeat of evil, but women scholars note that it is also a misogynist fantasy. And, as women scholars have also indicated, men exert control over these female figures. Women are not numbered in the 144,000 faithful of 14.4. Instead, women's bodies are objects of desire and violence, with the likelihood that women themselves are simultan-eously desired and feared. In fact, there is no female figure in the text that is not an archetype or a stereotype. Safety is only to be found in exile and the loneliness of the woman crowned with the sun who has fled to the desert after giving birth.

however, that fact of the importance of the two images concerned within the Revelation is manifest.

The 'Word' of God is, of course, a key concept in the Gospel according to John (1.1) and 1 John (1.1); it is no less central in the Revelation, but with a meaning closer to the usage in the Scriptures of Israel. The emphasis is on prophetic responsibility to speak the word of God, understood as parallel to the testimony of Jesus himself (Revelation 1.2–3, 9; 2.1, 8, 12, 18; 3.1, 7, 8, 14; 6.9; 17.17; 19.9; 20.4) and the very content of John's vision. Yet Jesus himself can also be portrayed as the conquering Word of God (19.13–14), 'King of kings and Lord of lords'. In this passage, the stark imagery of clothing bathed in blood is evidently drawn from Isaiah (63.2), and the term 'Word' owes a great deal to the Aramaic usage, *memra*, which is a highly dynamic concept, often referring to God's vindicating and punishing victory over the changeable attitudes of people. The rootedness of the Revelation in the usage of the Scriptures of Israel and their Aramaic translation is instanced in other examples as well, but this usage is perhaps the best indication of how the Revelation represents a precedent for 1 John and the Gospel, and how it represents a turn within a deeply Semitic tradition.

The Revelation's imagery of Jesus as the lamb that was slain is even more striking. John portrays the slain lamb at the very center of the divine throne, receiving heavenly worship (Revelation 5.6–14; 15.3; 22.3) and emanating divine wrath as well as ultimate blessing (Revelation 6.16; 14.10; 22.1). This lamb alone is designated as worthy to remove the seals of vision, a theme that is repeated with great emphasis (6.1–7). So potent is the power of the heavenly lamb, those who are martyred in Jesus' name are described as having washed themselves in the blood of the lamb, so as to worship him and to enjoy eternal salvation (7.9–17). Once developed, this becomes a signature theme until the close of the book (Revelation 12.11; 13.8; 14.1–4; 21.27).

Just as Jesus is the 'Word of God' in a way that accords with the usage of the Prophets and Judaic tradition, so also as the slain lamb of sacrifice can he be described as 'Lord of lords and King of kings' (Revelation 17.14), an appropriation of divine language to Jesus which is authorized by the content of John's vision of the lamb on the Throne itself. But because this lamb truly is Jesus, the imagery can shift radically, so that the lamb hosts a bridal feast (Revelation 19.9), at which he himself is the bridegroom. Within the eucharistic imagery, the bride is identified as the heavenly Jerusalem (21.9–10), the eternal Church on the foundation of 'the twelve apostles of the lamb' (21.14).

The ultimate power of the lamb, however, is shown by what he replaces in the heavenly Jerusalem of John's vision: 'I did not see a temple in the city, because the Lord God Almighty and the lamb are its temple' (Revelation 21.22–23). By a careful deployment of the temple image, therefore, which has been present since early in the book (see Revelation 3.12; 7.15; 11.1, 19; 14.15, 17; 15.5–8; 16.1, 17), the Revelation addresses the central question that had catalysed renewed apocalyptic visions within Judaism and Christianity alike. Now, visionary authority – complete with the insistence that no addition or subtraction should ever be made – mandated that no earthly temple should ever usurp the place of the lamb that was slain.

Together with its triumphant address of the central problem of apocalypse, taking up a position on visionary grounds that Hebrews had staked out on the basis of intellectual argument, the Revelation also correlates vision with other types of authority. It vindicates the language of 1 Peter in respect of the temple, but also the recourse of 2 Peter to the Prophets, the incarnational and sacramental emphasis of 1–3 John, and the insistence of Jude in regard to the eternal changelessness of faith. In the Revelation to John, vision is made the principal engine of knowing the will of God, but in a way that accommodates the aspirations of emerging, Catholic Christianity. How the relationship among different claims of authority and revelation worked out over the centuries has often been articulated by the way in which the Revelation to John has been interpreted. It is not an appendix to the New Testament, as it has sometimes been treated since the Enlightenment, but the capstone of a visionary tradition that runs through the entire tradition of the Bible.

Bibliographical background

Albert Schweitzer is rightly credited with making the issue of apocalyptic central to the study of the New Testament; see *The Quest of the Historical Jesus: A Critical Study of its Progress from Reimarus to Wrede* (tr. W. Montgomery; London: A. & C. Black, 1911). Even at the time of Schweitzer, however, Johannes Weiss argued that apocalyptic disclosure was less a matter of calendrical forecast than of comprehensive revelation; see *Jesus' Proclamation of the Kingdom of God* (tr. Richard Hyde Hiers and David Larrimore Holland; Philadelphia: Fortress, 1971). Progressively, the position of Weiss gained traction during the twentieth century, although an attempt – principally among British scholars – to reject eschatology and apocalyptic as central to the study of the New Testament did not carry the day. Among central or useful publications, see Paul S. Minear, *New Testament Apocalyptic*, Interpreting Biblical Texts (Nashville: Abingdon, 1981); Paul D. Hanson (ed.), *Visionaries and their Apocalypses*, Issues in Religion and Theology 4 (London: SPCK and Philadelphia: Fortress, 1983); Bruce Chilton (ed.), *The Kingdom of God in the Teaching of Jesus*, Issues in Religion and Theology 5 (London: SPCK and Philadelphia: Fortress, 1984); Ithamar Gruenwald, *From Apocalypticism to Gnosticism: Studies in Apocalypticism, Merkavah Mysticism and Gnosticism*, Beiträge zur Erforschung des Alten Testaments und des antiken Judentums 14 (Frankfurt am Main: Lang, 1988); James C. VanderKam and William Adler (eds), *The Jewish Apocalyptic Heritage in Early Christianity*, Compendia rerum Iudaicarum ad Novum Testamentum. Section 3, Jewish Traditions in Early Christian Literature 4 (Assen: Van Gorcum; Minneapolis: Fortress, 1996); Duane F. Watson (ed.), *The Intertexture of Apocalyptic Discourse in the New Testament*, Society of Biblical Literature Symposium Series 14 (Atlanta: Society of Biblical Literature, 2002); Scott M. Lewis, *What are They Saying about New Testament Apocalyptic?* (New York: Paulist Press, 2004); Edward Adams, *The Stars Will Fall from Heaven: Cosmic Catastrophe in the New Testament and its World*, Library of New Testament Studies 347 (London: T. &T. Clark, 2007); William C. Nicholas, Jr, *I Saw the World End: An Introduction to the Bible's Apocalyptic Literature* (New York: Paulist Press, 2007); Jonathan T. Pennington and Sean M. McDonough (eds), *Cosmology and New Testament Theology*, Library of New Testa-ment Studies 355 (London: T. &T. Clark, 2008); Albert L. Hogeterp, *Expectations of the End: A Comparative Traditio-historical Study of Eschatological, Apocalyptic and Messianic Ideas in the Dead Sea Scrolls and the New Testament*, Studies on the Texts of the Desert of Judah 83 (Leiden: Brill, 2009).

Awareness that apocalyptic opened up a range of questions about the fate of the world as well as personal experiences that were taken up by many of the last writers of the New Testament has led to analyses that deal with the issues across several documents. Among them feature A. J. Mattill, *Luke and the Last Things: A Perspective for the Understanding of Lukan Thought* (Dillsboro: Western North Carolina Press, 1979); Raymond E. Brown, *The Epistles of John*, The Anchor Bible 30 (Garden City: Doubleday, 1982); John T. Carroll, *Response to the End of History: Eschatology and Situation in Luke–Acts*, Society of Biblical Literature Dissertation Series 92 (Atlanta: Scholars Press, 1988); Andrew Chester and Ralph P. Martin, *The Theology of the Letters of James, Peter, and Jude*: New Testament Theology (Cambridge: Cambridge University Press, 1994); John M. Court, *The Book of Revelation and the Johannine Apocalyptic Tradition*, Journal for the Study of the New Testament Supplement Series 190 (Sheffield: Sheffield Academic Press, 2000); David R. Nienhuis, *Not by Paul Alone: The Formation of the Catholic Epistle Collection and the Christian Canon* (Waco: Baylor University Press, 2007).

Exercises

1. Apocalypticism

The texts of *4 Ezra*, *2 Baruch* and the Revelation are often described as 'apocalyptic' in their outlook. Read the text box about '*4 Ezra* and *2 Baruch*' on p. 143, and then answer the following questions.

Questions

1 What are the responses of *2 Baruch*, *4 Ezra* and the Revelation to the destruction of the Temple? (See e.g. Revelation 11.1–2; *4 Ezra* 9–10; *2 Baruch* 85.)

2 What are the characteristics of an apocalyptic worldview? (See Collins under Further reading.)

3 Are Jesus and Paul apocalyptic figures? (See, for example, Mark 9.1; Mark 13; 1 Corinthians 7.29–31.)

2. 2 Peter on Paul's letters

The author of 2 Peter cites Paul in support of the letter's argument about the coming judgment:

> So also our beloved brother Paul wrote to you according to the wisdom given him, speaking of this as he does in all his letters. There are some things in them hard to understand, which the ignorant and unstable twist to their own destruction, as they do the other scriptures. (2 Peter 3.15–16)

This allows us to conclude that 1 Peter post-dates Paul's letter-writing activity. The passage connects Paul's letters with 'other scriptures', implying inspiration but not necessarily canonical status.

Questions

1 What view of Paul and Paul's letters can be inferred from this passage?

2 How do you read the description 'all his letters'?

3 Who is appealing to Paul as an authority figure?

3. Acts

Acts is the only book in the New Testament that sets out to record the events immediately after the death and resurrection of Jesus. It is in the book of Acts that we learn Jesus' disciples were called 'Christians' for the first time at Antioch (Acts 11.26) as well as learning about important events such as Pentecost, the conversion of Paul and the mission to the Gentiles. Read the text box 'What type of book is Acts?' on p. 145 and what it says about the opening of Luke in the text box 'Gospel beginnings' on p. 105, then answer the following questions.

Questions

1 To what genre do you think Acts belongs?

   (a) Is it history? (See Acts 1.1–8.)

   (b) Do you think it has apocalyptic features? (See the text box on p. 154 for examples of other apocalyptic texts, and see Acts 2.)

2 Speeches are an important feature of Acts; can you identify them?

(a) What are the particular emphases of these speeches?
(b) What are their common elements?
(c) What meaning can be attributed to the speeches as a whole?
(d) To whom were the speeches directed?

3 Acts provides another source of information about the apostle Paul in addition to his letters.

(a) Compare the account of Paul's conversion in Acts (9.1–21) with what Paul says about his own conversion (Galatians 1.11–12).
(b) Compare what Acts says about Paul's preaching (Acts 14, 17) with what Paul says about his preaching (e.g. 1 Thessalonians 1.9; 1 Corinthians 2.1–5).
(c) What impression of Paul's character does Acts give? How does this compare with the impression of Paul we receive from his letters?
(d) How do you account for the differences?

4. Is the Revelation misogynist?

The Revelation to John is a revelation of the end. It begins with a vision of Christ to the seer John on the island of Patmos and continues with letters to seven churches in the western part of Asia Minor (modern Turkey). Thereafter the seer witnesses sequences of seven events: opening of the seven seals, blowing of seven trumpets, pouring of seven bowls. Read the text box on p. 154 and then answer the following questions.

Questions

1 Identify female figures and stereotypes in the Revelation. What is their fate?

2 Scholars writing on the Revelation argue that it depicts male violence between men and to women. How would you evaluate this argument in regard to the Revelation?

3 Is gendered violence intrinsic to a vision of apocalyptic power? (Begin by looking at other apocalyptic works mentioned in this chapter – see the exercise above on apocalypticism.)

Further reading

J. H. Charlesworth (ed.), *The Old Testament Pseudepigrapha*, 2 vols (New York: Doubleday, 1983, 1985)

J. J. Collins, *The Apocalyptic Imagination: An Introduction to Jewish Apocalyptic Literature* (Grand Rapids: Eerdmans, 1998)

Luke Timothy Johnson, *The Acts of the Apostles*, Sacra Pagina 5 (Collegeville, Minnesota: Liturgical Press, 1992)

Lee Martin McDonald, *The Biblical Canon: Its Origin, Transmission and Authority* (Peabody, Massachusetts: Hendrickson, 2007)

Sarah Parvis and Paul Foster (eds), *Justin Martyr and His Worlds* (Minneapolis: Fortress Press, 2007)

Tina Pippin, *Death and Desire: The Rhetoric of Gender in the Apocalypse of John* (Louisville, Kentucky: Westminster John Knox Press, 1992)

Marion L. Soards, *The Speeches in Acts: Their Content, Context and Concerns* (Louisville, Kentucky: Westminster John Knox Press, 1994)

Michael Stone, *Fourth Ezra*, Hermeneia Commentary Series (Minneapolis: Augsburg Fortress Press, 1990)

Glossary

Apocalyptic (adj.) and **apocalypse** (noun) derive from the Greek noun *apokalupsis*, revelation or uncovering of immanent and catastrophic events accompanying the end of the world and the birth of a new heaven and a new earth. In the biblical books of Daniel and the Revelation, visions given to a seer or prophet are written down.

Apocrypha, from the Greek 'hidden' or 'secret', includes additions to the Greek Bible (see Septuagint) and entirely new books like Tobit and the Wisdom of Solomon. Once thought to be hidden, these writings are now included in Scriptures of other Christian traditions and in publications of Old Testament and New Testament Apocrypha.

Aramaic was spoken and written throughout the Near East from *c.*600 B.C.E. to *c.*700 C.E. and was the major language of Palestine, Syria and Mesopotamia in the formative periods of Christianity and Rabbinic Judaism. Two of the major translation traditions of the Hebrew Bible – the Syriac Peshitta and the Jewish Targums – are in Aramaic, as are substantial portions of Rabbinic literature, the entire literary corpus of Syriac Christianity, and that of the Mandaeans (a non-Christian gnostic sect of southern Iraq in existence today).

Dead Sea Scrolls refers to the publication of Hebrew, Aramaic or Greek material from 11 caves at Qumran on the shores of the Dead Sea between 1947 and the mid 1960s, along with material from Judaean desert caves (Murraba'at, Hever, Se'elim, Mishmar), containing literature dating between the two Jewish Revolts (70 to 135 C.E.). This material has revolutionized our knowledge of Judaism in the Second Temple period and dramatically influenced the study of Christian origins. Versions of every book of the Bible except Esther have been found among the scrolls. All the biblical texts predate versions of the biblical text published in our Bibles.

Diaspora, or dispersion, refers to the dispersal of Jews throughout the Hellenistic world. Large Jewish communities existed in Rome from the second century B.C.E. and in Alexandria and Sardis from the third century B.C.E., for example.

Eschatology, from the Greek *eschaton* or last, describes last things, including life after death and judgment of souls.

Glossary

Eucharist, from the Greek word for thanksgiving, refers to the sacred meal in which gift of the body and blood of Christ is celebrated. The Eucharist was regarded as a sacrament in Christian churches from the third century C.E..

Essenes, a Jewish sect described by Josephus and the philosopher Philo of Alexandria existing, from the second century B.C.E. to the end of the Jewish War against Rome, (66–70 C.E.), on the shores of the Dead Sea. For many scholars, the Dead Sea Scrolls at Qumran are an Essene library.

Gnosticism derives from the Greek word *gnosis*, or knowledge, and is used (often pejoratively) by some scholars to describe a radically dualistic movement contemporaneous with Christianity in the first centuries of the Common Era. Other scholars have questioned whether the term is useful at all. Gnostic systems of thought view the world as the faulty creation of a fallen inferior god identified as the God of the Hebrew Bible. Recognizing themselves as mired in matter, Gnostics think that the goal of human existence is to ascend to the place of origin, the world above. Publication of the Nag Hammadi Library has increased our knowledge of this movement.

Hellenism. The Hellenistic world describes Greek thought and culture including and subsequent to Alexander the Great. After Alexander's death (323 B.C.E.) without an heir, his generals continued as Hellenistic rulers in Egypt (the Ptolemies, including Cleopatra) and Syria (the Seleucids, including Antiochus IV Epiphanes). The spread of Greek language and culture throughout the Mediterranean world resulted in the translation of the Hebrew Bible into Greek in the second century B.C.E. (see Septuagint). The New Testament itself is written in Greek.

Mammon, an Aramaic word for wealth or property, occurs in the phrase 'unrighteous mammon' (Luke 16.9, 11).

Miqvah (Heb. pl. **miqvaoth**) is a ritual washing to restore purity. In observance of ritual purity, the Pharisees drew on an old tradition of using priestly laws concerning purity, food and marriage in order to separate, protect and identify Judaism in the Graeco-Roman period.

Pseudepigrapha (Old Testament and New Testament) literally refers to a falsely titled work such as the book of *Enoch*, the *Ascension* or *Assumption of Moses*, since neither Enoch nor Moses were the authors of writings subsequently attributed to them.

Quelle, from the German word *quelle*, meaning source, is a conjectured sayings source used in the composition of the Gospels of Matthew

164

and Luke. While some scholars have published reconstructions of Q, others prefer to regard the sayings common to Matthew and Luke as fluid oral tradition.

Septuagint, from the Latin word for 70, refers to the translation of the Hebrew Bible into Greek by 70 translators in the third century B.C.E., according to a story reported in the Letter to Aristeas. This is the form of the Bible familiar to most New Testament authors and many Christians in the first few centuries of the Common Era.

Son of God, a term used by, for example, Paul to describe Jesus. In the Hebrew Bible (Old Testament) the term is used to describe the divine beings (angels) of Genesis 6 who visit human women on earth. In Psalm 2, God calls an anointed king of Israel 'son of God'. In Greek and Roman culture an individual human being, for example the Emperor, was called 'son of god'.

Son of Man is a term Jesus appears to use as a self-designation (e.g. Mark 2.10). Scholarly opinion is divided between the views that Jesus' use of the phrase is an Aramaic idiom for speaking about oneself in the third person, or a particular divine figure derived from the apocalyptic description of the Son of Man in Daniel 7.13–14.

Stoicism was a particular philosophy prominent in the Hellenistic period. The philosopher Zeno established the Stoic school, which lasted from 300 B.C.E. to the third century C.E.. The name derives from stoa, or pillars of the colonnade in Athens, where Zeno walked with fellow philosophers. In Stoic philosophy, an active principle, reason (*logos*), permeates the universe and is manifest in reason and human rational thought. In Stoic ethics, freedom from passions is the result of virtue. Elements of Stoic philosophy can be seen in Paul's thought.

Synoptic Gospels is a term describing the first three Gospels of the New Testament, Matthew, Mark and Luke, from the fact that since they have so much material in common, they can be seen together or alongside one another. A synopsis of the four Gospels publishes material from the Gospels in four parallel columns. Much of the material from John's Gospel exists without parallel in the Synoptic Gospels.

Targums (Heb. *Targumim* from the verb to translate or explain) are Aramaic translations and paraphrases of biblical Hebrew texts made for Aramaic-speaking Jews of the synagogues who no longer understood classical Hebrew. Eventually, under the direction of the rabbis, these were set down in writing.

Index